THE WORLDS OF

Jane Austen

Family tree

William Walter
+
Rebecca Hampson
+
William Austen
Thomas Leigh
+
Jane Walker
Grandparents
Grandparents
Uncle William
Aunt Philadelphia
Leonora
Rev. George Austen
+
Cassandra Leigh
Uncle James Leigh Perrot
+
Jane Cholmeley
Thomas
Aunt Jane
+
Edward Cooper
Parents
The Walter cousins
Cousin Eliza
James
George
Edward
Henry
Cassandra
Frank
Jane
Charles
Cousin Edward
Cousin Jane
Hastings
Anna & others
Fanny & others

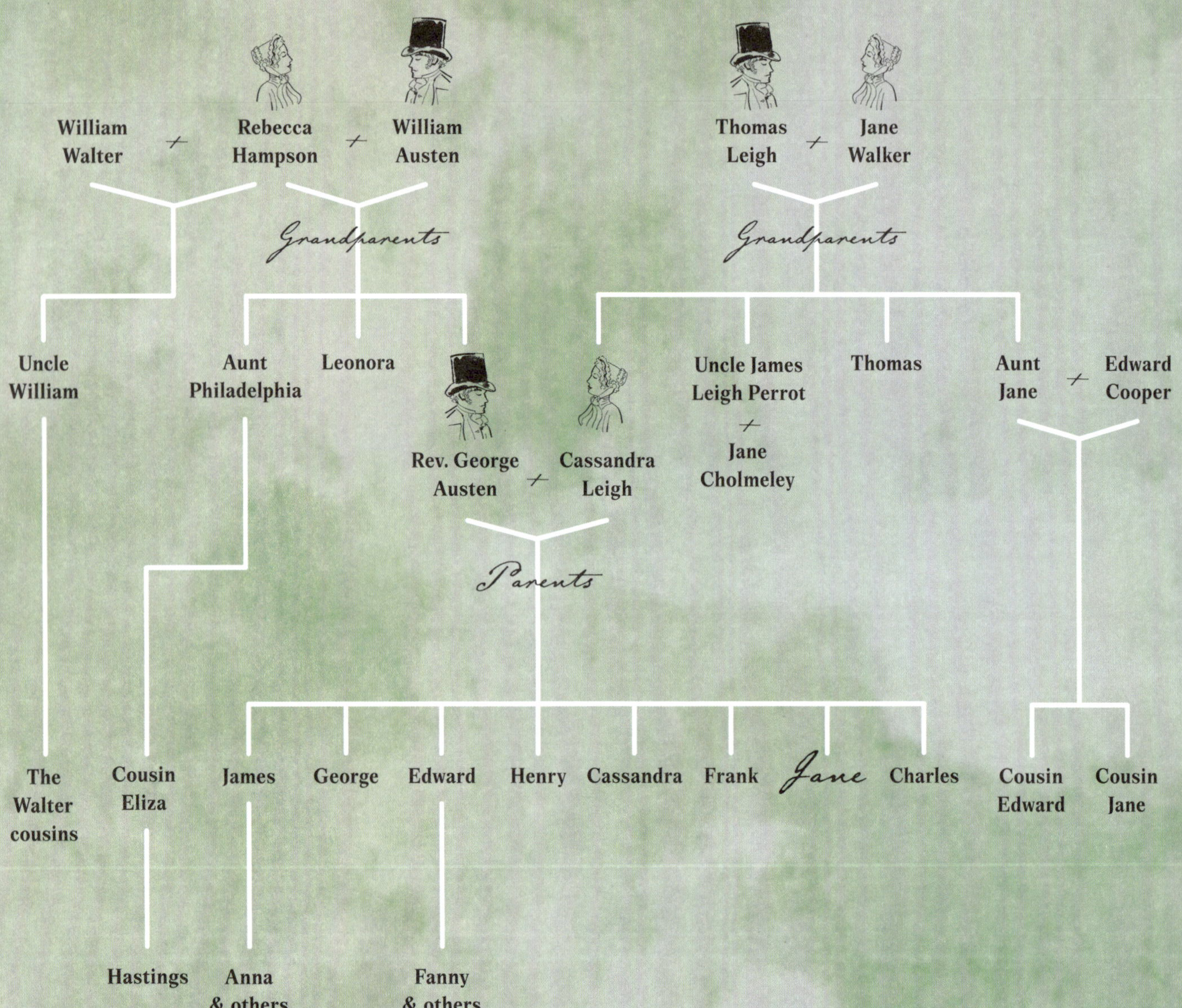

THE WORLDS OF *Jane Austen*

THE INFLUENCES AND INSPIRATION BEHIND THE NOVELS

Helena Kelly

Contents

The Rectory

'The house itself stood in a shallow valley, surrounded by sloping meadows, well-sprinkled with elm trees, at the end of a small village [...]' –

James Edward Austen-Leigh, *A Memoir of Jane Austen*

Nestled in a Hampshire valley, between softly rolling hills, sits the village of Steventon. Though the M3 motorway passes within a mile, and the town of Basingstoke has been creeping ever closer, Steventon feels as if it's in the middle of the countryside. The view is of fields and hedgerows, the lanes are narrow, and the village itself so small that, visiting for the first time, you may be unsure whether you really have arrived at your destination. Standing outside the quiet grey church of St Nicholas, its graveyard dominated by a vast, spreading yew tree, you can easily imagine that the door will open to reveal an eighteenth-century clergyman on his way to the rectory.

We have to rely on pictures and descriptions of the rectory that stood in Steventon in the eighteenth century, since the building itself no longer exists. But we know that on Saturday 16 December 1775, the rector's wife gave birth to a baby there: a little girl, her seventh child in eleven years. 'She is to be Jenny,' announced the proud father, in a letter written the next day to his sister-in-law. The world would come to know her as Jane Austen.

Convention dictated that mother and baby remain indoors, and preferably in bed, for a period; no hardship in this case, for the weather soon turned bitterly cold. The River Thames froze over. Livestock died of exposure. Possibly this explains why nearly four months went by before Jane was officially received into the church for the first time, much longer than was the case for any of her siblings; but it may be that she didn't thrive as expected, or that her mother took longer than normal to recover.

The image of the little village in the valley and of the rectory house, peacefully blanketed in snow, ties in with a vision of Jane Austen that still persists: that her life was uneventful, even dull; her world small, safe and narrow.

Opposite Jane Austen colourised picture after various illustrations derived from a c.1870 engraving, ultimately, after Cassandra Austen's unfinished portrait of her sister.

Left St Nicholas Church in Steventon, Hampshire, where Jane Austen's father presided.

Below Felix Octavius Carr Darley, *The Battle of Lexington*, 1877. One of the opening battles of the American Revolutionary War. Britain was at war for almost the whole of Jane Austen's life.

But 1775, the year Jane was born, is when the American Revolutionary War began. That war ended in 1783, when she was seven, with American independence from Britain. The French Revolution started in 1789, when she was just entering her teens. Then in 1793 Britain and France went to war. Jane was seventeen years old. Aside from a short period of peace in 1802–3, the two countries remained at war until she was nearly forty. There was a series of wars in India, and the War of 1812, between Britain and the United States. There were repeated invasion scares. In 1797 French armies tried to land in Wales, and they succeeded in landing in Ireland the following year.

Jane was not insulated from what was happening in the world. Two of her brothers were in the Royal Navy. Her French cousin-in-law was guillotined in Paris in 1794. The so-called Great Western Road, which ran from London to Bath and Exeter, passed about a mile to the west of Steventon. A mile in the opposite direction was

Left Daniel Thomas Egerton, *The Insolence of Office*, 1824. Before the advent of the railways, public stagecoaches offered transport around the country. One route ran close to Steventon.

Right Silhouettes of Reverend George Austen and Cassandra Austen née Leigh, Jane's parents.

Below right Henry Bone, *His R.H the Prince Regent*, 1816. The Prince, later George IV, rented a house close to Steventon and rode with the local hunt.

the turnpike road between the cathedral city of Winchester and the bustling town of Basingstoke – one of the fast main routes maintained by levying tolls on passing vehicles. In some of the short stories and poems that Jane wrote when she was young, she jokes about the proximity of these roads: in one sketch a traveller from Bath to London is delayed near Steventon, while a turnpike intrudes comically into an 'Ode to Pity'. But if the French *had* invaded along the south coast and marched on the capital, Steventon was probably not where you would have wanted to be.

It's true that it was small (there were only about twenty households). Old maps of the neighbourhood show fields and woods, other villages, farms and an occasional large mansion surrounded by parkland. But this part of Hampshire was considered good hunting country and was consequently fashionable – the Prince Regent, later George IV, rented an estate close to Steventon for several years in the 1790s. Jane's eldest brother rode with the same hunt as him. The majority of inhabitants worked on the land but there was a silk mill in Overton, the next village over, one of several factories forming a local textile industry. A short walk would have taken you from the rectory to either the Wheatsheaf Inn on the turnpike or the New Inn in Overton, where coaches passed daily, stopping to pick up and drop off passengers. Crimes took place in the area – theft, violent assault, highway robbery, arson. Visitors to the Austens included one aunt who had lived in India, and another from Barbados. Steventon wasn't a rural backwater. Nor was the rectory as restful or secure a household as you might assume.

By the time Jane was born, her father George Austen was rector of two parishes: Steventon and nearby Deane. He rented out the Deane parsonage house. He farmed, on a moderate scale. In addition to these income streams, he and his wife Cassandra Leigh had both inherited modest amounts of money, but they had seven other children besides Jane: James (born 1765), George (1766), Edward (1767), Henry (1771), Cassandra (1773), Francis ('Frank', 1774) and Charles (1779). University was not out of reach for the Austen boys, who, through their mother, were eligible for scholarships reserved for those who could prove they were related to the founder of St John's College Oxford, but a university education was in itself no guarantee of a successful and financially rewarding career. Then there were the girls to be considered. There was also George junior, the second of the Austen children, who, it was apparent from early on, would require lifelong care.

The outsiders

The treatment of Jane's maternal uncle Thomas Leigh and of her brother George Austen may well dismay modern readers. They were both sent to live with paid carers in Monk Sherborne, a village about eight miles from Steventon. George, we know, suffered from fits and had poor mobility; Thomas was probably intellectually disabled. There are indications that the income from shares which were held in trust for Thomas didn't always get to him intact, since Mrs Austen at one point appears to suggest giving a portion of it to one of her daughters-in-law instead. Both men survived into their seventies, however, so it seems that they were fairly well looked after. How frequent or extensive the contact between them and the rest of the family was is something we simply don't know. In a letter written to her sister in December 1808, Jane mentions an acquaintance who was 'totally deaf', to whom she 'talked [...] a little with my fingers' and this is sometimes seized on as evidence that she was accustomed to using sign language with her brother, but we have no idea how much – if any – time they actually did spend together.

Such behaviour was unfortunately not unheard of, though the prevalence of poor obstetric treatment, childhood disease and late-in-life pregnancy meant that disabilities were very common. There's some reason to believe that Jane's aunt Leonora Austen may also have required additional care. Leonora didn't die until 1783, but she is seldom mentioned in family correspondence. She had ended up living with distant connections in London, to whom her sister Philadelphia paid regular sums of money, and there's no indication she visited her brother at the rectory in Steventon.

Less dismaying is the experience of young Hastings de Feuillide, the son of Jane's cousin Eliza and – after Eliza married Henry Austen – her step-nephew. Hastings's difficulties (possibly indicative of cerebral palsy) were quite severe and his health was often poor, but he remained at home until his tragically early death. He was of course the only child in a well-off family rather than one of many in a household where money was tight, but the difference is marked.

In the 1830s, Jane's richest brother, Edward, made a point of transferring the money left to him by his mother to George, who hadn't been mentioned in the will, suggesting that he at least had reservations about the way his brother had been treated.

Dubious legacies

More than one character in Austen's fiction makes a marriage which displeases their relations and it seems that her paternal grandparents may well have done the same in real life. After his apprenticeship in Woolwich, to the east of London, Jane's grandfather, William Austen, had returned to his home town of Tonbridge in order to establish himself as a surgeon. There he encountered Rebecca Walter. She was about seven or eight years his senior, well into her thirties, with a child. She was also recently widowed.

In January 1728, the couple married – not in Tonbridge, but in London. Until the middle of the eighteenth century a legal quirk meant that you could marry cheaply, speedily and quietly, without banns or a wedding licence, in certain areas of the capital, such as the environs of the Fleet Prison. Thousands of people did exactly that every year. The fact that William and Rebecca's first child was baptized just eight months after their wedding suggests that speed may have been their primary motivation. They may also have wished to avoid protests from their respective families. There was a considerable age gap, and a gap in social status.

Rebecca's father, Sir George Hampson, had been a baronet, though he hadn't succeeded until his children were grown up. Her sisters had married rich men, however; her brother, another George, now held the title. William Austen had been born into relative affluence, but debt, the early death of his father and the indifference of his grandfather had seen his status plummet. Rebecca died in 1733 and her husband four years later, after an ill-thought-out remarriage which left his three young children homeless. Still, in spite of their considerable wealth, the Hampson family remained unwilling to provide much in the way of practical help.

Rebecca's son from her first marriage was apprenticed to a mercer, a cloth merchant, in Tonbridge. Philadelphia may have been cared for by connections of her mother before being apprenticed to a London-based milliner (hatmaker). Meanwhile, George Austen and his youngest sister Leonora were left to their father's family.

In her novel *Mansfield Park*, Jane explores a similar situation, contrasting the experience of a girl whose mother had 'married in the common phrase, to disoblige her family' with that of her affluent cousins, children of a baronet. Marrying without the support and approval of your relations could, she knew, have long-lasting consequences, reaching down the generations.

Previous John Nost Sartorius, *Fox Hunting: Gone Away*, 1787. Riding to hounds was a popular rural sport and several of Jane Austen's brothers took part in it.

Right Emil Brac, detail from *Die Geografiestunde* (*The Geography Lesson*), 1905. The work offers a fair idea of what the schoolroom at Steventon Rectory might have looked like.

There was little scope for sentiment. Mrs Austen made a habit of weaning her babies early and then handing them over to foster parents, only receiving them back at the rectory when they were more manageable. George junior was at some point during his childhood sent away permanently. The two youngest Austen boys, Frank and Charles, were on active service in the Royal Navy by their early teens. Jane and her sister Cassandra, aged seven and ten respectively, were dispatched to a boarding school where, according to family lore, both nearly died. A short time later they were enrolled at a different one.

Clergymen often provided private tuition to the offspring of well-off neighbours, but it was less usual to do what the Austens did, and set up a small boarding school in their own home, welcoming boys from further afield and educating them alongside their own sons. It meant that Jane grew up in a house with a piano, plenty of music, more than 200 books, a 'terrestrial globe' and even a microscope – all advertised for sale in the *Reading Mercury* in April 1801, when the Austens moved. However, the imposition on domestic and family life must have been considerable. Terms were long. Mr Austen had to remain always in the role of teacher and disciplinarian; Mrs Austen in that of school matron and housemistress. The pupils didn't just provide income, though; they were themselves an investment, a network of rich or influential acquaintances and connections that the family might be able to draw on in the future.

The rectory was definitely a busy house, then, and for many years a place of business, full of people. Jane's parents were, by modern standards, neglectful, and even by the standards of their own time briskly practical. The village in which Jane spent most of her youth was small but it wasn't either idyllic or isolated.

Left Jean-Baptiste Van Loo Augusta, *Princess of Wales with Members of her Family and Household*, 1739. One of Jane Austen's great aunts served as a bedchamber attendant to Augusta, mother of George III. The position was considered a great honour.

Right Thomas Rowlandson, *The dance of death: the Apothecary*, 1816. Several apothecaries are mentioned in Jane Austen's fiction, with Mr Perry, in *Emma*, being the most prominent. Her great-uncle was an apothecary in Tonbridge.

Exactly where the Austens belonged socially is harder to define. One of Jane's great-aunts was bedchamber attendant to George III's mother. It's possible to find quite a few titles on the outer reaches of the family tree: baronets, lords, even dukes. It's also possible to find attorneys, a bookseller, surgeons and an apothecary. Apothecaries were druggists providing basic, cheap medical care, while surgeons were only one step up and spent a lot of their time pulling out rotten teeth. These were not high-status careers and didn't require university training; they were trades, the kind of occupations that Austen's less pleasant characters sneer about. It was quite unusual at the time to find a social range as wide as this within one family. There's a reason why

Jane can write convincingly about everyone from noblewomen to hired nurses, businessmen to baronets.

There were several estates, some of them large, belonging to cousins and uncles. There was a lot of money floating around. However, a combination of factors had drawn almost all these resources away from Jane's branch of the family. Jane's grandfather had been all but disinherited, with family property and money being funnelled to his eldest brother, and he had made two rather imprudent marriages. Her father, George, and his sisters, Philadelphia and Leonora, had been left orphans, dependent on the sometimes grudging charity of their aunts and uncles, and their own wits. Jane's uncle James, her mother's brother, was rich; Jane's mother was not.

Living in the rectory house, children of a Church of England clergyman, the Austens were gentry. Remove the rectory, though, and their status would become much shakier. Jane grew up knowing this. In 1792, when she wasn't quite seventeen, she wrote several chapters of a novel, called *Catherine, or the Bower.* In it, the heroine's two best friends, daughters of a clergyman, have to move away after his death and one is obliged to become a 'companion' to rich relations – not quite a servant, but also very possibly not paid. Jane probably imagined that she might be married by the time her own father died and her home vanished. But when she was twenty-five, and still single, the reverend George Austen decided to retire, hand the rectory house over to his eldest son, sell the furniture, the piano and the books, and relocate. According to family tradition, Jane shortly afterwards accepted a marriage proposal, only to change her mind the next morning. There followed a profoundly unsettled period of nearly a decade, during which her father passed away, and she and her sister and mother drifted from place to place – travelling to coastal resorts, to Bath and London and Kent, paying visits to relations, and for a time setting up home in Southampton. A family story suggests that during one visit to the seaside she fell in love with a man who afterwards died; no further details have ever emerged. She is also often supposed to have fallen in love, when a young woman, with a man called Tom Lefroy. Nothing came of either relationship.

Jane had started writing when she was about twelve. We have her notebooks, in which several pieces are dated: you can see her rapidly improving as an author, moving from childish jokes to far more ambitious and sophisticated projects. When she was twenty-one, her father offered one of her manuscripts to a publishing house – usually presumed to be a work referred to as *First Impressions*, which may be an early version of *Pride and Prejudice*. It was turned down. Another manuscript was accepted for publication in 1803, but for some reason didn't appear. This was called *Susan* and, so far as we can tell, it was completely unrelated to Austen's story *Lady Susan*, being instead a version of *Northanger Abbey*. Whether she wrote anything new during the years when she was moving about remains a mystery still.

Jane was, for most of her life, financially dependent on others, and though her mother and sister had some income of their own, they remained heavily reliant on the generosity of their male relatives to help them maintain middle-class respectability. They must have been aware that there was no guarantee that generosity would continue indefinitely. Henry Austen had found his way into banking, still a fairly new career then and a risky one: in 1816 his bank did in fact collapse, taking with it money belonging to several members of his family. Jane lost a relatively small amount but other, richer, relatives lost thousands. Frank and Charles, the naval brothers, were as dependent on patronage and luck as on their own skill and courage. They were away for long periods of time, facing significant dangers at sea. Fortunately, there was Edward, who had the good fortune to catch the fancy of rich, childless, distant cousins. He eventually came into possession of their property, which included one estate in Kent and another in Hampshire, in a small village called Chawton, close to the town of Alton. In 1809, Jane, her sister and their mother moved there, settling into a large red-brick cottage which Edward had done up for them. It was opposite the duck pond and fronted straight on to a busy road, so that when the coaches went past, the windows rattled in their frames, but it offered Jane the stability that seems to have been so crucial to her work.

She was in no position to refuse the many requests her family made of her – nursing, childcare, counselling her older nieces out of unwise romantic attachments. But once she was at Chawton, she turned serious attention to her writing. In 1811, she published *Sense and Sensibility*; in 1813, *Pride and Prejudice*. The following year it was the turn of *Mansfield Park*, and the year after that, *Emma*. She lived to see her work favourably reviewed and to receive royal approval, being invited to dedicate a novel to the Prince Regent. Before she died, in 1817, she had written *Persuasion*, revised *Northanger Abbey* and started what's now known as *Sanditon*.

It's easy to wish that Jane had gone to live at Chawton sooner, or that her adult life had been more stable. But her experience of insecurity is one of the things that makes her novels so powerful. We're moved, reading about the Dashwood sisters being exiled from their family home in *Sense and Sensibility*, and about Mrs Bennet's fear that she will be unable to support

Tom Lefroy

In 2021, the Honresfield Collection, a mass of papers by important British authors, was saved for the nation. It included poems in Emily Brontë's own handwriting. It also included a letter written by Jane Austen to her sister, in January 1796, when she was just twenty, which mentioned a young man named Tom Lefroy. Austen scholars were beside themselves with excitement. Not only was this the earliest surviving letter written by Jane, but all three of the actual physical letters in which Tom is referred to had been essentially missing, unseen for decades, their whereabouts uncertain. To discover even one of them was a coup.

Tom is sometimes identified as the love of Jane's life and has been claimed as the inspiration behind several of her novels. As an elderly man, he apparently admitted to having harboured a 'boyish' love for her – he was actually only nineteen when they met, a few weeks younger than she was. Exciting as the re-emergence of the letter was, however, it isn't clear that it shows us Jane in love. Indeed, there's an argument for saying that the more serious her feelings for Tom, the less likely we'd be to know anything about him: Jane's correspondence was repeatedly culled by her relatives, the worst offender probably being her sister Cassandra. When Jane was older, she frequently joked about male admiration where it's obvious it didn't exist, but though she does joke about Tom, it seems that there may well have been a genuine – and mutual – attraction. She brings him up several times in the letter, noting that he has almost the same birthday as Cassandra, saying that they have demonstrated to other couples 'how to be particular' at dances, mocking his coat which is 'a great deal too light', his 'one fault'. He is, she writes, 'a very gentlemanlike, good-looking, pleasant young man'.

There may have been gossip about the pair, because Jane reassures Cassandra that they have only seen each other at dances, and that he is 'so excessively laughed at about me [...] that he [...] ran away when we called'.

The second letter, which we have only from an early transcription, states that an acquaintance drew a picture of Tom to give to Jane. It also contains a sardonic claim that Jane's 'tears flow as I write, at the melancholy idea' that 'the Day is come on which I am to flirt my last with Tom Lefroy'. Assuming that the transcription of the third letter is correct, the only other reference comes nearly three years later and is to the effect that Jane was 'too proud to make enquiries' about Tom. Altogether it's suggestive but rather scant material.

Tom's uncle was married to a woman who claimed to be a distant cousin of Jane's, and was a dear friend. Even once Jane had moved away, and Tom's uncle and aunt were both dead, their relatives remained near neighbours. In 1814, Jane's niece Anna married Tom's cousin Benjamin Lefroy. Jane would have known that Tom had married the daughter of a merchant; she'd have heard about the arrival of his children and the progress of his legal career. Whether she pined for him, or quickly learned to laugh about their youthful dalliance, she wouldn't ever have been able to forget him entirely.

Above Portrait miniature of Tom Lefroy, by George Engleheart. Portraits were often commissioned to mark an occasion such as marriage or coming of age, so this may show Tom at the time Jane knew him.

Left A silhouette marking Edward Austen's adoption by the Knights, by William Wellings, 1783. This was less formal than a modern legal adoption. While being brought up as the heir of the Knights, Edward also continued to be considered part of his birth family.

her children in *Pride and Prejudice*. Part of the reason we're moved is because although this is fiction, it draws on real feelings.

As far as we know, Jane never went as far north even as Birmingham. The only other country she may have visited is Wales, and we are not certain she did that. She sets her novels in places that she knew, and she fills them with the kinds of people she encountered in real life. But she didn't just know rectory houses; she knew cramped city lodgings and seaside holiday rentals and spacious estates. Her acquaintance wasn't limited to clergymen; she knew sailors and soldiers, lawyers, school teachers and slave owners. When she wrote about characters thrust suddenly into new and unfamiliar surroundings, about rich, capricious relatives, about poorly written wills, ill-advised marriages and sibling estrangements, she didn't need to invent: she could find inspiration in what had happened in her own family.

But she was also inspired by what was going on beyond her family circle: a culture in ferment, a world convulsed by war. Her life was not a long one – December 1775 to summer 1817, only just over forty years – but it saw extraordinary changes: the emergence of new countries and new political movements, the fall and rise of empires. Science and technology, religion, literature, even the landscape of Britain. Almost nothing remained untouched.

No Popery
Death or Liberty & No Popery

Revolution

'Here was another strange revolution [...]'

Mansfield Park

Historians sometimes talk about the late eighteenth and early nineteenth centuries – Jane Austen's lifetime – as the Age of Revolutions. By this they don't mean just the American or French or Haitian revolutions, the rebellions in Russia and South America, or more localized unrest like the Gordon Riots, which shook London in 1780, and the 1798 uprising in Ireland. There were other titanic shifts taking place as well.

In the 1760s westerners were still talking about 'Terra Australis', the semi-mythical southern continent. By the end of the 1780s, Britain had set up a prison colony in Botany Bay, in what's now Sydney. Jane's brother Frank Austen served under Captain Isaac Smith, who was reportedly the first person to go ashore at Botany Bay in 1770. China was in an expansionist mood, as was Russia. European colonial powers claimed huge areas of territory in India and Africa and the Americas, which they then fought over, or sold, or bargained away in treaties. In 1803, less than thirty years after it had first come into being, the United States doubled in size overnight after 'buying' millions of acres from France – land which three years before had (nominally, at least) been under Spanish control. The mapmakers couldn't keep up.

The British Isles were changing too. In 1801, partly in response to the uprising which had taken place a few years earlier, Ireland was officially united with Britain. Enclosures, which reorganized rural spaces to enable larger-scale, more intensive agriculture, started to become ever more popular as new methods of farming, new crops and new breeds appeared. With a population that had grown by 15 per cent between the first census, in 1801, and the second, in 1811, it was seen as vital to produce as much food as possible. Millions of acres were enclosed during Jane's lifetime.

Opposite Henry Roberts, detail from *An Exact Representation of the Burning, Plundering and Destruction of Newgate by the Rioters on the memorable 7th of June 1780*, 1871.

Top right J. Prockter, *A correct map of the world drawn from the best discoveries*, c.1760. Only parts of the coastline of Australia are shown.

Below right Samuel Calvert, *Captain Cook taking possession of the Australian continent on behalf of the British Crown, AD 1770*, later nineteenth century, after John Alexander Gilfillan.

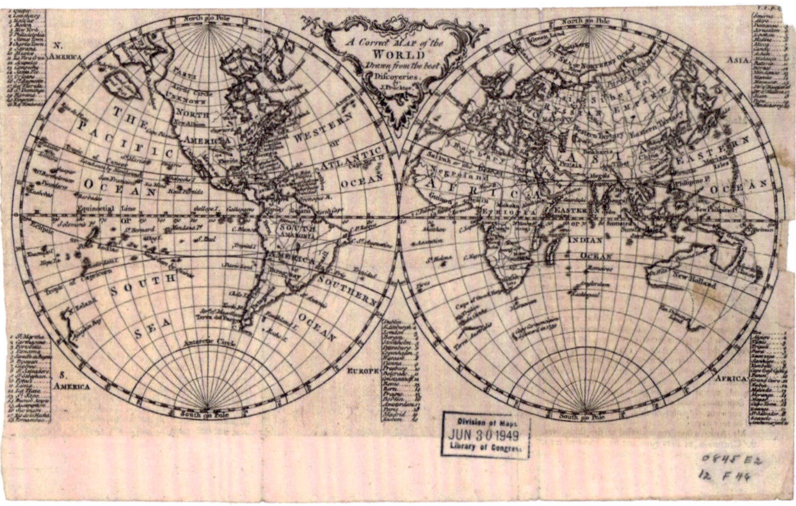

Hedges and fences went up; footpaths were shut off. Traditionally, people had been permitted to find firewood and trap rabbits and perhaps pasture a cow in open common spaces. Once an enclosure had been completed, this was no longer possible: the common space was gone and serious hardship sometimes resulted. Jane saw two enclosures up close, and refers to the process in several of her novels. It's clear, for example, that the area around Highbury, the setting for *Emma*, has recently been enclosed.

At the same time, technological innovations were arriving thick and fast. New telescopes enabled the discovery of the planet Uranus and of comets and nebulae. Better furnaces produced cast iron and steel fit for ever more advanced projects. 'Manufactories' sprang up, making textiles and tools and china and dyes. A network of canals was constructed to move raw materials and finished goods around the country. As the 1770s turned into the 1780s, steam engines were deployed – cautiously at first, and then more widely. There were accidents, but by the end of the 1790s, steam power was no longer seen as a novelty. By the 1810s steamboats were beginning to puff their way down the eastern side of Britain, and back and forth across the Irish Sea. There were a number operating on the River Thames during Jane's lifetime. In the 1780s, humans took to the skies for the first time in hot-air balloons.

Technology doesn't feature prominently in Jane Austen's fiction, but she does seem to have been aware of it. The governess in *Mansfield Park* takes care that her pupils should know about 'all the Metals and Semi-Metals'. In *Pride and Prejudice*, Elizabeth Bennet is invited to take a trip to the Lake District with her aunt and uncle. She envisages spending her time amid 'rocks and mountains' but in the event, they only get as far as

Lunatics and geniuses

The Lunar Society was a loose grouping of intellectuals and innovators based around Birmingham. It included people like the astronomer William Herschel, the chemist Joseph Priestley, the potter Josiah Wedgwood and James Watt, an engineer who pioneered more efficient steam engines (and for whom the unit of power is named). Also linked to it were men who are now better known for their descendants: Erasmus Darwin, Charles Darwin's grandfather, and Richard Lovell Edgeworth, whose eldest daughter, Maria, became an extremely successful novelist and was much admired by Jane Austen.

Around these figures, and their overlapping social and family circles, it's possible to see something recognizably like the modern world beginning to take shape. Jane's cousin Edward Cooper, who was a clergyman, lived for many years at a parish in Staffordshire and found himself on the edges of some of those circles. In August 1806 Jane paid him a visit: more evidence, if needed, of her proximity to new and disruptive ideas.

Below Joseph Wright, detail from *A Philosopher Giving that Lecture on an Orrery, in which a Lamp is put in place of the Sun*, 1766.

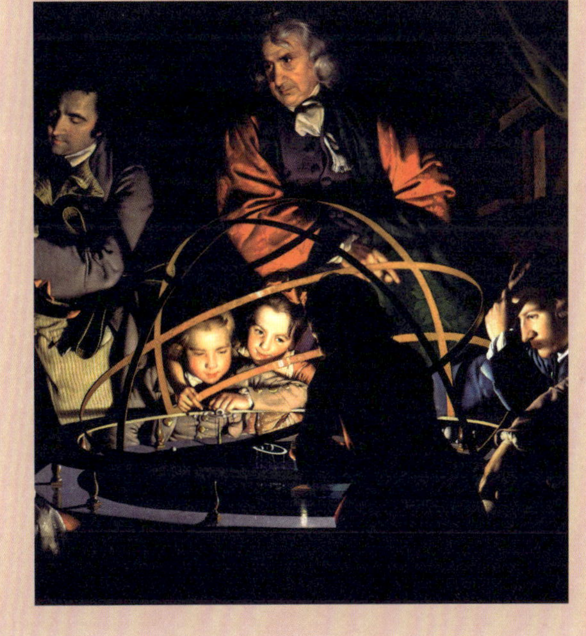

Above *The Comet*. Launched in 1812, this combined wind power and steam and was designed to operate along the River Clyde, in Scotland, as a passenger ship.

Right Boulton and Watt's Soho Foundry, Birmingham, late 1790s. During Austen's lifetime Birmingham was a centre of technological innovation. Elizabeth Bennet visits the town on her way to Derbyshire in *Pride and Prejudice*.

Right William Shuter, *William Wordsworth*, 1798. *The Lyrical Ballads*, written by Wordsworth and his friend Samuel Taylor Coleridge, were considered so innovative that they were accompanied by a long explanatory essay.

Derbyshire, travelling, we're told, via Birmingham, which was famous at the time for its factories and as a centre of mass production. The town also hosted many meetings of the Lunar Society.

This episode encapsulates one of the significant differences between Jane Austen and the Romantic poets who were her near contemporaries – people like William Wordsworth and Samuel Taylor Coleridge – whose work is sometimes seen as rejecting or evading the Industrial Revolution. They write seriously about rocks and mountains, and mystical, spiritual experiences in nature, while Jane seldom lets her characters get very far into their rhapsodies on stars or shrubs, or the bittersweet beauties of autumn, without poking fun at them. It's probable the contrast is deliberate, because we know she kept up with trends in poetry. By the time we get to *Persuasion*, and a scene set in 1814, the characters are discussing *Marmion* and *The Lady of the Lake*, popular Scottish history poems by Sir Walter Scott, and enthusing over Lord Byron. Jane herself seems not to have succumbed to Byron mania, however. Though she read Byron's *The Corsair* in March 1814, within a few weeks of its publication, she merely noted, in a letter to her sister, that she had finished it, without expressing any opinion.

It's difficult for us to understand how exciting and astonishing, how revolutionary, some of this poetry appeared at the time. For much of the eighteenth century, Scottish culture had been repressed, for the simple reason that Scotland was so closely associated with the Stuart dynasty. There had been several failed rebellions in support of the Stuart ambition to take back the British throne from the House of Hanover. The last of these, in 1745–6, had been the most successful, with troops taking over the Scottish capital and then

Right *Prise de la Bastille en 1789* (*The Storming of the Bastille in 1789*). The French revolution inspired British radicals and terrified more conservative thinkers.

marching several hundred miles into England, before a decisive defeat at the Battle of Culloden. The Stuart cause was effectively finished by the end of the century, though many – particularly in Scotland – maintained a lingering affection for it. Stuart monarchs feature in both *The Lady of the Lake* and *Marmion*. Byron's poems not only included passages which were fairly sexually explicit, but they also made immorality look glamorous. Wordsworth felt it necessary to include a 10,000-word essay as a preface to his *Lyrical Ballads,* explaining what he was trying to achieve and defending his focus on 'subjects from common life' and use of 'language near to the real language of men'.

Even putting the Stuarts and what Wordsworth, in his preface, had termed 'revolutions in literature' to one side, a good deal of literature published during Austen's lifetime would probably have been seen as revolutionary anyway.

The American Revolution had been talked about in Britain, and written about, but it never dominated the political and cultural landscape in the way the French Revolution did. From the symbolic storming of the Bastille prison onwards, the events of 1789 captured the British imagination, and they didn't let go.

France was the old enemy. It was Catholic. It had an absolute monarchy, with no effective controls on the power of the king – unlike Britain – and continued to practise imprisonment without trial. During the Seven Years War of 1756–63 Britain and France had battled across the globe. They'd not long finished fighting each other in India. Despite this, conservative British thinkers lined up to defend the French king and queen, Louis XVI and Marie Antoinette, and criticize the revolutionaries. Liberals, meanwhile, eagerly hailed a new age of freedom, equality and brotherhood.

Opposite John Jones, *Edmund Burke*, c.1790. Burke was a politician, author of the *Reflections on the Revolution in France*, and mover in the impeachment of Warren Hastings, an acquaintance of the Austens.

Below King George III, *Studio of Sir William Beechey*, c.1800.

A number travelled from Britain to France to get a ringside seat. It was, after all, not very far to go. Hundreds of publications about the revolution appeared, ranging from religious sermons to furious *ad hominem* attacks, poetry to dry philosophical treatises.

The dominant conservative voice was that of Edmund Burke, whose *Reflections on the Revolution in France* rejected the idea that reform was even possible. Fiddle with one part of the established order, he suggested, and the entire structure would come to pieces. For Burke, it was 'natural' and proper to cling to what he called the 'old prejudices': to 'look up with awe to kings, with affection to parliaments, with duty to magistrates, with reverence to priests, and with respect to nobility'. Only firm pressure from above could keep everything together and everyone in their rightful place. Without it, there would be chaos.

There was, of course, one quite obvious problem with Burke's argument: in 1788 George III had suffered from a serious illness that left him mentally incapacitated for a period. This problem certainly recurred again afterwards and may have happened before. There's no definite consensus on what the illness was, but the two suggestions which carry the most weight are either something called porphyria – where various chemicals accumulate in the body, producing a variety of damaging symptoms – or bipolar disorder. The king's difficulties had been widely reported on. It wasn't a secret: people knew that he had been 'mad', unfit to govern. He wasn't the best advertisement for the traditional security offered by a monarch.

One rapid response to Burke came from Mary Wollstonecraft – famous nowadays both for her feminism and for her daughter Mary Shelley, the author of *Frankenstein*. Her *A Vindication of the Rights of Men*

Right The title page of the American edition of Mary Wollstonecraft's *A Vindication of the Rights of Woman*, 1792. An early feminist text.

Opposite John Opie, detail of *Mary Wollstonecraft*, 1797.

'Bliss was it in that dawn to be alive,
But to be young was very heaven'

The Prelude, William Wordsworth

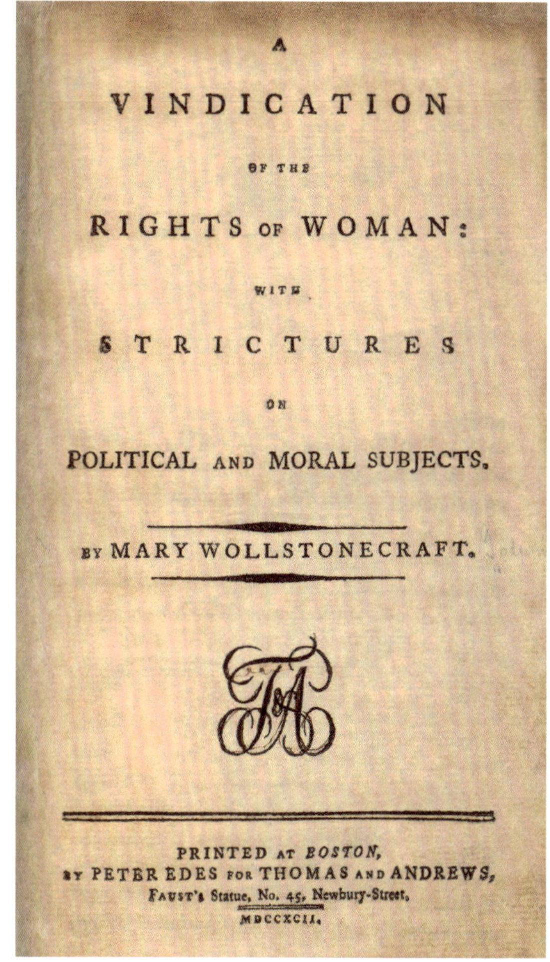

A

VINDICATION

OF THE

RIGHTS OF WOMAN:

WITH

STRICTURES

ON

POLITICAL AND MORAL SUBJECTS.

BY MARY WOLLSTONECRAFT.

PRINTED AT BOSTON,
BY PETER EDES FOR THOMAS AND ANDREWS,
FAUST's Statue, No. 45, Newbury-Street,
MDCCXCII.

was overshadowed, however, by the extraordinary success of Thomas Paine's *Rights of Man*, which sold hundreds of thousands of copies and saw its author – and his publishers and booksellers – prosecuted for 'seditious libel' (that is, treasonable writing or printing).

The prosecution was part of a government crackdown driven by the fear that revolution was about to spread to Britain. Printers and booksellers were intimidated. Letters were intercepted. Individuals were spied on and informers recruited. But liberal authors kept writing and they could still find some publishers willing to support them. In 1792 Wollstonecraft followed her attack on Burke's *Reflections* with *A Vindication of the Rights of Woman*, now hailed as one of the founding texts of British feminism. In 1793 William Godwin published *An Enquiry Concerning Political Justice*, which argued that in an ideal society founded on reason, all power structures from monarchy to marriage would prove unnecessary and wither away. Samuel Taylor Coleridge and his friend Robert Southey, another politically radical poet, made serious plans to set up a commune, either in America or (more prosaically) in Wales, where all property and labour was to be shared equally. Coleridge embraced anarchism and atheism. Southey published *Wat Tyler*, which centred on the mediaeval Peasants' Revolt against the nobility, and poetry collections which highlighted the hard lives of the contemporary labouring poor. Yet, given how many copies of the *Rights of Man* there were, and how many radical societies, there were surprisingly few prosecutions for sedition and treason, and not many of those were successful – juries chose to acquit. The government view was not shared by everyone.

Years later, William Wordsworth remembered how thrilling this time had been: 'Bliss was it in that dawn

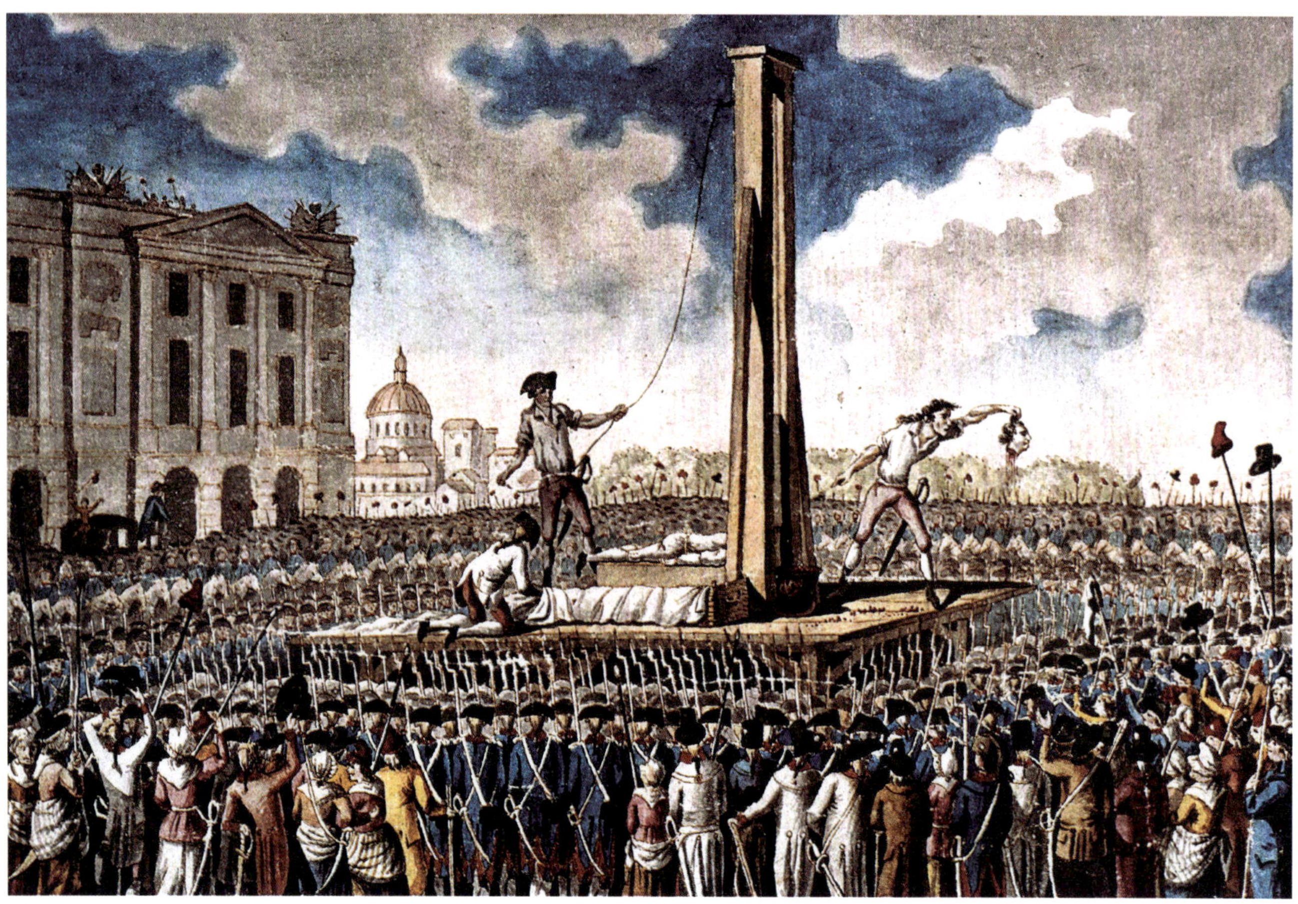

to be alive,' he wrote, in his autobiographical poem *The Prelude*, 'But to be young was very heaven'. Jane Austen was a little younger than Wordsworth and Coleridge, but she was young in the same dawn as them. Like them, she arrived at intellectual maturity during a period when the old, established ways of living and thinking were being dismantled, when change seemed to be not just within reach, but irresistible, inevitable. She lived through the backlash as well.

The French revolutionary leaders successfully resisted aggression from Austria and Prussia. They set up a republic. They reformed the calendar and also killed the man who had been their king, beheaded their former queen, declared war on Britain, and turned on each other. During the months of the so-called *Terreur* (Reign of Terror), a shocking 17,000 official executions took place. Among that number was a man called Jean-François Capot de Feuillide, the husband of Jane Austen's cousin, Eliza, who learned that she was a widow from a list of deaths printed in a newspaper.

These brutal excesses shook many liberal thinkers. There was no putting the genie back in the bottle, however. The British government passed new treason laws in 1795, which made almost all political gatherings or meetings illegal, but rioting against food shortages continued through the second half of the decade. Naval mutinies broke out at Portsmouth and at the Nore, the sandbank anchorage in the Thames Estuary. A crowd threw stones at the king's carriage. In 1796 a group known as the United Irishmen planned a revolution and invited French troops to help them. The plan only failed because of terrible weather. Eighteen months later,

Opposite *Fin Tragique de Louis XVI* (*The Tragic End of Louis XVI*), c.1793, print after what was supposedly a drawing from the life by an artist called Fious.

Above Isaac Cruikshank, *The Delegates in Council or Beggars on Horseback*, 1797. A political cartoon depicting the Nore mutineers and suggesting the involvement of several radical politicians, who are shown lurking under the table.

in 1798, the United Irishmen did take up arms and this time the French soldiers landed. Fighting continued across Ireland for several months before the uprising was finally subdued.

For most of the 1790s, the British government was scared, and it had good reason to be. Everywhere it looked, danger was visible: France on one side, Ireland on the other. In the countryside, increasing numbers were being impoverished and alienated by enclosures. Population growth and industrialization had swelled the towns and cities, and produced the perfect conditions for political agitation and mob violence.

Women couldn't vote, and neither could most men. Large landowners were often in a position to simply choose the members of parliament for their districts. Some of the most densely populated towns in the

Previous Thomas Robinson, *The Battle of Ballynahinch*, c.1800.

Right Isaac Cruikshank's *The Rival Pigs*, 1795, depicts the conservative prime minister William Pitt and the radical Charles James Fox as pigs, but also shows the marked difference in their hairstyles.

country had no representation in the House of Commons. People found other ways of expressing and identifying political allegiances. The songs you sang, the publications you read, your opinions on poaching or enclosure or slavery, or the position of women or the conduct of the war – almost everything became politicized. Once a tax had been levied on hair powder, even hairstyles were politically charged. Using powder meant you were a government supporter, while cutting your hair short and leaving it natural suggested that you might harbour revolutionary sympathies.

Most people were not, to start off with at least, entirely on one side. Many were liberal on some topics and more conservative on others, or driven by personal or local sympathies. Many changed their minds or attempted to occupy a middle ground. But as often happens in culture wars, those in the middle found themselves attacked on two fronts. As the 1790s wore on, two camps emerged, and you were either in one or the other. The things that people said and wrote then continued to affect their lives for decades afterwards. By the time Robert Southey was made Poet Laureate in 1813, he had been a government supporter for years, but the newspapers still made sarcastic reference to his 'old Sonnets to Liberty'. In 1817, his radical poem *Wat Tyler* was reprinted without his permission and extracts were read out in parliament. Impatient at being simultaneously portrayed as a dangerous fifth columnist and a hypocrite, Southey pointed out that he had merely grown up and changed his mind, but people had long memories.

We have three notebooks filled with stories and plays and poems that Jane Austen wrote between the end of the 1780s and beginning of the 1790s, when she was entering her teens. In one story called *Henry and Eliza*, the heroine makes an enemy of a 'Dutchess', who throws her into prison without trial. Having escaped, we're told that she 'raised an army', 'entirely demolished' the Duchess's prison, 'and by that act, gained the Blessing of thousands'. This looks at first as if it must have been inspired by the storming of the Bastille. But it looks, equally, as if it must have been a very early work, written when Jane was thirteen or fourteen; it's sometimes been argued that it dates to 1788, when she would have been twelve and, of course, before the Bastille had been attacked, though Newgate Prison in London had been broken open during the Gordon Riots of 1780. Either way, it's a rollicking, comical adventure, which probably doesn't have much to tell us about the author's political opinions.

The overall flavour of these early works is unmistakably anarchic, though. Children defy the 'Shackles of Parental Authority' as a point of principle. Women get 'dead drunk', leave their babies in haystacks or run away with lovers. There are secret marriages and divorces, violence, thefts, murders and any number of elopements. One heroine gobbles down six ice creams and then knocks the shop proprietor over rather than paying. A minor character has her leg broken in a mantrap. In *Love and Freindship* [sic] two young women leave a trail of destruction all over Britain, acquiring and abandoning husbands, running up debt and stealing money. There are plenty of characters with titles but they are even stupider and vainer, more lascivious and violent than anybody else. Sir George and Lady Harcourt are introduced in the act of beating their

Opposite Thomas Lawrence, *William Pitt*, 1807; a posthumous portrait.

idle haymakers with 'a cudgel'. The elderly, debauched Lord St Clair is alarmed to find himself suddenly encountering no fewer than four grandchildren, offspring of the illegitimate daughters he fathered on a mistress, and considers he has fulfilled 'the Duty of a Grandfather' by giving them each a £50 note.

Royalty doesn't do much better. Jane's short attempt at non-fiction – *The History of England: From the reign of Henry the 4th to the death of Charles the 1st. By a partial, prejudiced, and ignorant Historian* – includes stringent criticisms. One monarch is described as a 'Monster of Iniquity and Avarice'. Several connive at murder. Henry VIII's 'only merit' lies in 'not being quite so bad as his daughter Elizabeth', while she is a 'disgrace to society' and 'pest to humanity'. Dated November 1791, just before Jane's sixteenth birthday, the tone hovers uneasily between childish silliness and mature irony.

Jane warns the reader at the beginning that her work will include 'very few' dates. Confessing that she does not 'perfectly recollect' all the events that took place during the reign of Henry VIII, she contents herself with writing mostly about 'Anna Bullen' (Anne Boleyn) and Catherine Howard. She expresses a decided bias in favour of the Stuarts and says that she is 'partial to the roman catholic religion'. These are not altogether serious statements, but they're also not apolitical.

The History covers an extremely violent period of time in English history. It begins and ends with a king who is murdered (Richard II and Charles I respectively). In between, a number of other royals are killed. There are two civil wars. Jane refers elliptically to the behaviour of 'roman catholics' towards 'the Royal family and both Houses of Parliament' during the reign of James I. She means the Gunpowder Plot of 1605, when conspirators planned to blow up the House of Lords, the House of Commons and the King on 5 November. It is possible to see all of this as a response to Burke's *Reflections*: a sardonic riposte to his assertion that the English have traditionally looked up with awe to kings and affection to parliaments; a challenge to his argument that monarchy offers stability and security.

We might, again, be seeing something that isn't there, though. *Catherine, or the Bower*, written a little less than a year later, in August 1792, appears to be Jane's first serious attempt at a novel and it has no real engagement with current affairs. We're told that people discuss 'Politics' but the discussions are so generic that they could almost appear with minimal editing in any fiction written between 1700 and 2000. One character has been in France and we're left to assume that the revolution can't have taken place yet, because no one refers to it, even obliquely. 'Mr Pitt', the prime minister, is mentioned only in passing, so glancingly that it's easy to miss.

Catherine is a short fragment; it's very difficult to work out what Jane was intending to do. It's possible that she didn't know herself, or that events, at home or in the wider world, scuppered her plans. But there are three finished novels which, it is widely believed, started life around the middle or towards the end of the 1790s, though they were only published later on: *Northanger Abbey*, *Sense and Sensibility* and *Pride and Prejudice*. The titles look rather different when placed alongside Burke and Mary Wollstonecraft, and viewed against the backdrop of that revolutionary decade.

Wollstonecraft's *A Vindication of the Rights of Woman* includes several lengthy discussions of 'sensibility' – cultivated emotional sensitivity. Society, Wollstonecraft suggests, sees sensibility as desirable in women, but in her opinion it is dangerous, increasing their vulnerability to both sexual feelings and depression.

Redemption
of the
National
Debt

'[...] after some deliberation he chose Fordyce's Sermons [...] and [...] with very monotonous solemnity, read three pages'

Pride and Prejudice

In one of these discussions there's a passage where Wollstonecraft asks her readers to consider the plight of a girl or girls 'left by their parents without any provision', dependent on the 'bounty' of a brother. The brother may have a 'habitual affection' towards his sisters, but his 'cold-hearted, narrow-minded' wife will be 'jealous of the little kindness which her husband shews [sic] to his relations' and use every means at her disposal to ensure that they are 'worked out of her home'. This is very similar to what happens at the beginning of *Sense and Sensibility*. Having come into almost the entirety of the family property, even the 'cold-hearted' John Dashwood initially harbours relatively generous intentions towards his step-mother and half-sisters, who have been deprived of any proper 'provision' – until, that is, his 'narrow-minded' wife talks him down to giving them nothing, over the course of a few pages, and soon afterwards makes it impossible for them to remain living in the same neighbourhood.

Later on, Wollstonecraft writes at length about her disapproval of 'Dr Fordyce's sermons'. These were not religious sermons; she's talking about James Fordyce's *Sermons to Young Women*, a pompous, poorly reasoned and inexplicably popular book of essays about how teenage girls should behave, first published in 1766 and still selling as late as the 1830s. Since Jane has the ridiculous Mr Collins choose this same text to read aloud to his Bennet cousins in *Pride and Prejudice*, we are probably justified in thinking that her opinion of it cannot have been all that favourable either.

'Pride and prejudice' (or 'prejudice and pride') was a standard formulation during the late eighteenth century, much like the common toast, 'love and friendship', which Jane used as a title for one of her teenage fictions. Jane seems to have liked exploring

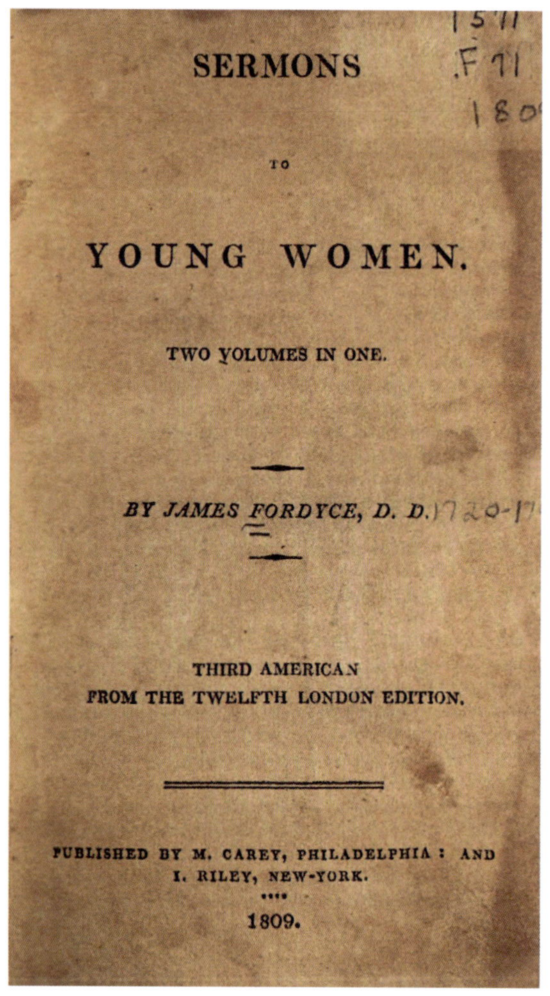

SERMONS

TO

YOUNG WOMEN.

TWO VOLUMES IN ONE.

BY JAMES FORDYCE, D. D.

THIRD AMERICAN

FROM THE TWELFTH LONDON EDITION.

PUBLISHED BY M. CAREY, PHILADELPHIA: AND I. RILEY, NEW-YORK.

1809.

Below The title page for an American edition of James Fordyce's *Sermons to Young Women*, published in 1809. The book details how girls should behave and Mr Collins chooses it to read aloud to his cousins in *Pride and Prejudice*.

phrases like this, ones which have been repeated so often that their meaning risks being lost. In one early scene in *Pride and Prejudice* she has some of her characters discuss pride in relation to the snobbish, standoffish behaviour of Mr Darcy at the local assembly rooms. They bat different ideas back and forth: is Darcy's high opinion of himself justified or excessive? Is it legitimate, showing proper discernment, or is it damaging to other people and to social cohesion? How is pride different from vanity?

There is no equivalent scene where the characters discuss prejudice, but in the 1790s one of its chief meanings was the one that Edmund Burke had given it at the beginning of the decade in his *Reflections*. For Burke, 'prejudices' were the knowledge of former generations distilled down and preserved. Prejudices were to be cherished, not questioned. Fearing God, looking up with 'awe to kings, with affection to parliaments, with duty to magistrates, with reverence to priests, and with respect to nobility' were 'inbred sentiments', 'natural', 'untaught feelings' sanctioned by time and use. In the summer of 1797, during a House of Commons debate about political reform, the radical MP Charles James Fox spoke of the 'pride and prejudice' which stood in opposition to his suggested constitutional 'remedies', and his speech was widely quoted in newspapers. It was, in a way, a political term. Jane didn't make it less political by attaching it to a novel in which the clergyman Mr Collins is treated with scant reverence, and the nobility – in the person of the disagreeable Lady Catherine de Bourgh, daughter of an earl – demands respect while doing very little to earn it.

Northanger Abbey is a slighter and lighter work, but still shows its author's awareness of the ideas and anxieties which dominated the 1790s. There is some amusing confusion about a riot. A young man aims to entertain a pretty young woman with a 'short disquisition on the state of the nation' while his father stays up late reading political pamphlets.

These are novels which mention enclosures and 'government' and refugees from the French Revolution. Just like in Jane's earlier stories, young people frequently defy their parents, and they're sometimes right to do so. Mothers and fathers can prove ill-tempered and ill-judging, controlling or downright negligent. And Jane presents a view of sex and marriage which at times is almost as bleak as Wollstonecraft's. Men who marry without paying due attention to intellect and character find themselves tied to pretty but perfectly brainless wives. Women with money of their own are targeted by fortune hunters; women without it may find themselves seduced and cast aside. There is no superior social class who can be relied on to keep order. Riches and titles are no guarantee of moral rectitude. On more than one occasion it's the lower-status characters who emerge either materially or morally triumphant in Austen. The poorly connected, ill-educated Lucy Steele ends up with a rich and malleable husband. Lizzy defies Lady Catherine and gets Darcy. The most admirable characters in any of these three 1790s novels are Lizzy's uncle and aunt – the former being the son of a country attorney who has gone into trade in London.

These are disruptive stories growing from a disruptive time – a time of revolutionary shifts and warring ideas.

Army and Navy

'[...] the young man wanted only regimentals to make him completely charming.'

Pride and Prejudice

Britain fought for nearly all of Jane Austen's life, at sea and on almost every landmass: in North and South America, India, the Caribbean, Africa, Europe, and even around the fringes of the Russian and Ottoman Empires.

There was no general conscription – not even during the height of the Napoleonic Wars, when the navy employed around 150,000 men and the army well over 200,000 – but this isn't to say that everyone serving in the armed forces had chosen to be there. The ranks were sometimes bulked out with convicted criminals. Individuals with sailing experience could be forced to serve in the navy; they could in fact be effectively kidnapped from civilian ships or off the streets by press gangs. In the popular ballad *Will Clewline*, a press gang seizes a man from his own home. Other ballads, like *Arthur McBride* or *Jenny's Complaint*, express hostility to the recruiting officers who tried to encourage young men into signing up as soldiers for the army. Jenny's love is made drunk by soldiers and forced to swear the oath. In what is clearly fantasy, Arthur and his cousin beat up the sergeant and get away.

Recruiters no doubt employed sharp practices, but many soldiers and sailors had volunteered – they were paid for doing so. For the navy that could sometimes be a generous lump sum, as much as £25 or £30 – more than a year's income. According to the historian Philip Henry Stanhope, Lord Wellington – general of the British army, and later prime minister – was famously scathing about soldiers' motives for signing up. 'People talk,' he is quoted as saying, 'of their enlisting from their fine military feeling – all stuff – no such thing.

Opposite Robert Home, *Arthur Wellesley, 1st Duke of Wellington*, 1804. This portrait predates his victories in the Napoleonic Wars.

Below The opening verses of 'Jenny's Complaint', a popular ballad lamenting questionable army recruitment tactics.

Opposite James Gillray, *Supplementary Militia, Turning-Out for Twenty days Amusement*, 1796. This seems to hint at several competing anxieties about militias; not only are the men mostly underfed and ill-equipped for a fight, but one wears a green 'liberty cap', a form of headgear associated with French revolutionaries.

Some of our men enlist from having got [i.e. fathered] bastard children – some for minor offences – many more for drink'. Men were liable to pay maintenance for their illegitimate offspring, and some will have been evading this or escaping otherwise uncongenial circumstances at home. For others, the prospect of regular pay and a pension may have looked increasingly attractive as the population rose and the cost of living with it, and the economy struggled to adjust to a triple whammy of enclosure, industrialization and war.

There was little chance of promotion from the ranks. Even the most able ordinary soldier would be lucky to make sergeant. Officers in the regular army were usually from well-off backgrounds, because the way you became an officer was by buying your way in. Once you were in, it was possible to advance on merit, or through knowing the right people, but there was every chance that someone with less experience but more money than you would suddenly become your superior. There were agents who sold commissions or brokered exchanges. Posts were advertised in the newspapers. At the end of *Pride and Prejudice*, Darcy buys Wickham an ensign's commission. An ensigncy, the most junior officer rank, cost several hundred pounds. This is at a time when the average agricultural labourer probably didn't earn as much as £20 in a year. Senior army positions were proportionately more expensive, and the cavalry was pricier than the infantry.

Though, for most of the novel, Wickham has been serving as a lieutenant in the militia, the ensigncy in the regular army is a step up. Militia officers didn't have to buy their ranks, only provide fairly modest sureties, and so it was a cheap option, open to those in less affluent circumstances like Wickham and, for that matter, Henry Austen. One of the jokes in *Pride and Prejudice*

60 CUMBERLAND BALLADS.

The sheep 'll nit ken Watty's voice now. The peat-stack we us'd to lake roun 'll be brunt ere this! As for Nan, she'll be owther married or broken-hearted; but, sud aw be weel at Croglin, we'll ha'e feastin, fiddlin, dancin, drinkin, singin, and smuikin, aye, till aw's blue about us:

Amang aw our neybors sec wonders I'll tell,
But niver mair leave my auld friends or the Fell.

January 10, 1803.

JENNY'S COMPLAINT.

TUNE—"*Nancy's to the greenwood gane.*"

O LASS! I've fearfu' news to tell!
What thinks te's come owre Jemmy?
The sowdgers hev e'en pick'd him up,
And sent him far, far frae me:
To Carel he set off wi' wheat;
Them ill reed-cwoated fellows[28]
Suin wil'd him in—then meade him drunk,
He'd better geane to th' gallows.

The varra seet o' his cockade
It set us aw a-crying;
For me, I fairly fainted tweyce,
Tou may think that was tryin:
My fadder wad ha'e paid the smart,
And show'd a gowden guinea,
But, lack-a-day! he'd kiss'd the buik,
And that 'll e'en kill Jenny.

"'I remember the time when I liked a red coat myself very well – and indeed so I do still at my heart'"

Pride and Prejudice

is that the pushy Mrs Bennet, blinded by the glamour of a 'red coat', doesn't fully appreciate the difference between a militia regiment and a regular one.

Militias were designed for internal security within the British Isles. There were unlikely to be many glorious victories, and besides – as a disruptive presence in the neighbourhoods where they were billeted, and a visible sign of state power – militias were sometimes a focus for resentment. They were permitted to conscript and did so by lottery, but it was possible to evade the lot by paying; there were a number of insurance schemes which, for a relatively modest sum, would permit you to do so, passing the job on to someone else. The result was that militias often comprised a large number of men who were well aware that the tough life they were leading in barracks or camps ought by rights to have been somebody else's. Extra militia strength was raised throughout the 1790s in response to the threat of invasion from France and the political unrest which was spreading at home, but given the recruitment practices, not to mention the harsh discipline soldiers were subjected to, it's unsurprising that the rank and file sometimes proved rather sympathetic to revolutionary ideas.

This was the case with the Oxfordshire Militia, the regiment that Jane's brother Henry Austen joined as a lieutenant in 1793. In April 1795 it mutinied, marching on Seaford and Newhaven – towns on the south coast, between Brighton and Eastbourne. Soldiers seized flour and provisions, stole horses,

Opposite James Northcote, *Admiral Sir Edward Pellew*, 1804. Pellew's success was prodigious and he garnered many titles and awards. He was made Viscount Exmouth for his successful attack on Algiers in 1816.

Left The execution of two of the leaders of the Oxfordshire Militia mutiny. Jane's brother Henry was a lieutenant in the Oxfordshires.

took control of a ship anchored in the river and got very drunk. They were subdued by regular troops sent out from Brighton. Two of the mutineers were hanged. In June, the entire regiment was made to watch while the ringleaders kneeled on the edges of their own coffins and a squad of a dozen men, chosen from among those who had been active in the mutiny, shot them.

In *Pride and Prejudice* the Bennet girls become very friendly with the militia officers who are quartered in the nearby town for the winter. They dance and dine and play cards together. Later in the novel the regiment removes to a summer camp in Brighton. Lydia, invited to accompany the colonel's youthful wife, imagines she will encounter orderly lines of tents and handsome young men in uniform: a cheerful vision that is perhaps somewhat overshadowed by the real-life behaviour of Henry Austen's regiment. The Oxfordshires, eager to dissociate themselves from the mutiny, were afterwards rather obtrusively loyal, and by the end of the decade were considered sufficiently reliable to be sent to serve in Ireland to help to stamp out the last flickers of the attempted uprising. There were many other militia regiments, though.

Pride and Prejudice is not a ringing endorsement of the militia or its officers, despite Jane's brother Henry spending nearly a decade as one. Nor do many of her other fictional soldiers come across well. The presumably retired General Tilney in *Northanger Abbey* is an unpleasant, ill-tempered individual, obsessed with rank and money. His eldest son, Captain Tilney, a cavalry officer, openly flirts with an engaged woman. *Emma* refers briefly to some more pleasant military characters, but we don't meet them. We see very little of Darcy's cousin Colonel Fitzwilliam, but the most significant thing he does is to gossip. There's Colonel Brandon, in *Sense and Sensibility*, but his army service has been in India, which, as we'll see, carried particular – and largely very negative – connotations.

Right *Royal Naval Academy, Portsmouth: panoramic view with an anchor*, after I.T. Lee, 1806. Jane's brothers Frank and Charles both attended the academy.

Below George Cruikshank, *The Sailor's Description of a Chase & Capture*, 1822, after John Sheringham. The hope of prize money was a strong motivation for sailors.

Right A daguerrotype, often identified as being of Frank Austen, Jane Austen's brother, who lived until 1865 and rose to become Admiral of the Fleet.

The navy meets with much kinder treatment. Jane's prominent naval characters are almost uniformly charming, from the eager young midshipman in *Mansfield Park* to the bluff and kindly admiral in *Persuasion*. They are brave yet modest, natural and unaffected, open-hearted and generous. Less positive is the portrayal of the father of the heroine of *Mansfield Park*: a loud, rough, overly physical 'lieutenant of marines' – marines being soldiers who were posted on board some larger navy ships. Even he, though, can moderate his behaviour when he wants to. Jane does mention a dim junior naval officer and a senior one whose home life is not all that it should be, but these are both minor, off-stage figures. Her keen eye never deserts her entirely, but it's clear that she admired her seagoing brothers.

The British Navy grew in popularity during the Napoleonic Wars, in spite of the increase in the hated press-ganging. The navy won quite frequently, and its wins were often both straightforward and spectacular – sink an enemy ship, or tow it behind you into port, and it's obvious that you have triumphed. Horatio Nelson was not the only sailor to become a household name. There was Admiral Pellew, who in 1797 disabled the French ship *Droits de l'Homme* (Rights of Man), which subsequently sank. There was Thomas Cochrane, the main model for the dashing Jack Aubrey in Patrick O'Brian's *Master and Commander* books. At sea, in ship-to-ship combat, the bravery and skill of individuals could and did make the difference between victory and defeat.

Naval careers started early. It wasn't impossible for boys to become midshipmen (the most junior officer rank) before they had hit puberty. Though there was an academy at Portsmouth – which Jane's brothers Frank and Charles both attended – it was not the favoured route to take. The feeling in the navy was that nothing was as valuable as experience at sea. Start young enough and everything would become second nature, from the calculations that helped you to work out your ship's position to which sails to set in any given combination of circumstances and weather. After six years at sea (or four, if entering from the academy) midshipmen were eligible to sit the examination for lieutenant, but even if they passed, they might languish unpromoted for years, unless they could find a captain willing to take them on. This is precisely what happens to the heroine's brother in *Mansfield Park* until her admirer, who comes from a navy family, finds the young man a position as lieutenant in order to ingratiate himself with her. While it wasn't possible to buy rank

Left Francis Chesham, *The capture of La Tribune by HMS Unicorn, 8 June 1796*, 1797, after Nicholas Pocock. Thomas Williams, who captained the *Unicorn*, was married to Jane Austen's cousin, Jane Cooper, and Charles Austen was on board as a midshipman.

in the navy, the system was not meritocratic. Class mattered, as did race. A range of different nationalities and ethnicities are represented in the crews of Royal Navy ships of the period, but the same cannot be said of the officers.

Patronage remained vital until you 'made post' – took command of your first ship after being promoted to captain. Once you had been 'posted', and had your name published in the *London Gazette*, you worked your way steadily up in seniority as those ahead of you died or moved up themselves. If you lived long enough, you would become an admiral. Charles Austen, who lived to the age of seventy-three, reached the rank of Rear Admiral. By the time Frank Austen died in 1865, he was ninety-one and had arrived at the very top, Admiral of the Fleet. But even once you had made post, favour and influence continued to determine who received the most desirable jobs. Blockade duty off the French port of Brest, in Brittany, was both dull and difficult, for example, whereas being sent to harass enemy shipping might make your fortune, and a brilliant victory net you a title – one of Jane's cousins became Lady Williams when her husband was knighted for capturing a French frigate.

But even the most successful captain or best-connected lieutenant would from time to time find himself without a ship, on half pay, while a lull in hostilities would, as one character puts it in *Persuasion*, '"turn [...] all our [...] Navy Officers ashore"' at once.

Life at sea was hard, particularly if you found yourself serving under officers who were less admirable than Jane Austen's fictional ones. You might be sent off to North America or the Indian Ocean and be away for years at a time, with news of family and friends taking months to arrive, or not reaching you at all. Discipline was tough. Minor infractions resulted in flogging.

For major ones, such as mutiny, the punishment was hanging. By the 1790s, sailors were supposed to be given lemon juice to combat scurvy, but it wasn't always sufficient. On long voyages, fresh food quickly ran out. Salted meat, stored in barrels, was often bad. Hard biscuits were usually full of weevils.
A proportion of the crew might have been abducted and forced to come on board, and with crowded quarters and disease, even those who had volunteered must have regretted their decision from time to time.

Fighting at sea must have been terrifying. There was nowhere to hide. Anyone on deck was vulnerable to enemy sniper fire. Below deck, cannonballs tore through hulls and bulkheads, throwing up shards of wood, each as lethal as a bullet. Cannons could misfire, or come loose. Get in the way of their recoil and you'd probably break a leg. If the gunpowder store was hit, the ship could explode. If an enemy crew boarded, there might be hundreds of men fighting and dying on a deck area smaller than a swimming pool. And all of this while at the mercy of the elements, with the added risk of drowning or of the ship sinking.

There was an incentive, however. If your ship succeeded in destroying or capturing an enemy ship, you received a share of the financial reward, a practice which continued up to the end of the First World War. The amount was dependent on several factors and varied according to rank, so that an admiral or captain would receive a much larger proportion than a midshipman, and a midshipman more than an ordinary sailor, but everyone got something. What was even more lucrative was to capture an enemy merchant ship or whaling vessel, because the reward pot would usually include the value of the goods on board, as well as the boat itself. There were also financial incentives for rescuing British merchant vessels from the enemy.

Opposite George Cruikshank, *The Point of Honour*, 1825. A crew assembles to see a flogging.

Left *A Greenwich Pensioner with a wooden leg, standing in a landscape, the domes of Greenwich Hospital behind*, 1813. Injury rates among servicemen were high.

This 'prize money' is how Captain Wentworth, in *Persuasion*, has acquired his twenty five thousand pounds – by a combination of honourable, if bloody, conflict, and what is arguably a form of glorified piracy. Many governments did officially license piracy at the time: 'letters of marque' were privateers holding certificates that allowed them to pursue enemy merchant vessels. Banning the practice for ships in the Royal Navy would have made it even harder for them to recruit men; the hope of a rich prize – and generous rewards for all – was a far more powerful inducement than patriotism. When Captain Wentworth discourses on his experiences, he mentions storms, his commands and his colleagues, but he also talks about 'taking' ships and 'how fast' he 'made money', and of his 'luck' off the West Indies and in the Mediterranean.

Captain Wentworth has indeed been lucky. Not everyone who fought for Britain was so fortunate. The numbers killed and injured during Jane's lifetime ran into the tens of thousands. Then there were those who died of disease or infection, or accident or drowning; those who paid the price for mutiny, or were flogged for some lesser offence. Add in the men who were too poor to evade the militia draft and the sailors taken from their homes, and in some parts of the country there would have been few families who remained unaffected.

Regiments, whether regular or militia, were seldom billeted in one place for very long. But wherever they were and whatever they were doing – be that marching to new quarters, completing training exercises or fraternizing with local women – they were visible. They were intended to be visible: part of their job, especially in the 1790s and during the early years of the nineteenth century, was to discourage rioters and would-be revolutionaries. Newspapers reported troop movements – just as they reported the arrival and departure of navy ships and listed promotions – and reproduced, word for word, dispatches from the front line. With so much of the fighting happening in Europe, news travelled fast and rumours even faster.

Britain was never occupied during the Napoleonic Wars and save for a brief, abortive French landing in Wales in 1797, it was not invaded either, but the civilian population was aware of and involved in the war in a way it hadn't been before. The presence of all those soldiers and sailors in Jane Austen's novels illustrates how much the war came to dominate everyday life.

Give a Girl an Education

"'Give a girl an education and introduce her properly into the world, and ten to one but she has the means of settling well, without farther expense to anybody'"

Mansfield Park

Education was not compulsory in Britain until the end of the nineteenth century and during Jane's lifetime there were plenty of people who received no schooling whatsoever. Annabella Millbanke, who would later marry the poet Lord Byron, was educated to near university standard in mathematics and science by a Cambridge fellow, but for every Annabella there were thousands of other girls who stopped at French and piano playing, and tens of thousands who got no further than reading, writing and simple arithmetic. Since the literacy rate in 1800 is usually quoted as 60 per cent for men and just 40 per cent for women, even this fairly basic level of formal learning was enough to put them in a minority.

There were moves to widen access to education. Most modern British Sunday schools are wholly religious, but when they first became popular towards the end of the eighteenth century, it wasn't unusual for them to offer several hours of free, formal lessons every weekend, and even to include subjects far removed from Bible study, like arithmetic or shoe-making. Some welcomed members of any congregation. There were also charity schools for both boys and girls, which would funnel children towards respectable jobs. In the absence of any state schooling programmes, though, opportunities like this remained a question of luck and geography.

Opposite Walker & Boutall, *Miss Millbanke*, 1812, after Charles Hayter. Anne Isabella (Annabella), Lady Byron received an exceptional education at a time when only about half the population was literate.

'Fanny could read, work, and write, but she had been taught nothing more'

Mansfield Park

Left A pupil at St George's Charity School for Girls in Southwark.

Opposite Frederick George Cotman, *The Dame School*, 1887. Though romanticised this is not an inaccurate image.

There were more options available for those who could afford to make a financial contribution towards their children's education. It was commonplace to outsource early years care and learning to nursemaids and to the emerging class of 'nursery governesses', who were much less well-qualified and thus much cheaper than those who catered for older children. There were 'dame schools', so-called because they were often run by women. These were plentiful, affordable and usually open to both sexes. They offered basic lessons and were roughly the equivalent of elementary school. Boys, when they were older, might be able to attend a nearby grammar school, where they would be treated to a curriculum heavy on Latin and Greek, intended as preparation for university. Usually set up by local philanthropists, grammar schools were part-subsidized and not expensive. There were also private schools, which offered a similar syllabus, as well as an increasing number of what were sometimes styled 'commercial' or 'mathematical' schools, which prepared boys for more practical careers with lessons in, for example, book-keeping, surveying and navigation.

Women did work during Austen's lifetime and not just as servants or manual labourers. They were artists, musicians, writers, translators, governesses, companions, dressmakers, milliners, nurses and midwives. They ran schools and businesses. One Mrs Martin set up the library in Basingstoke, which the Austen family used. But the career for which almost all girls were intended – and educated – was marriage.

Given this, it might seem strange that so much time and energy was dedicated to what might be called ornamental acquirements, rather than useful domestic ones, and that, for women at least, being well educated was synonymous with being 'accomplished'. In *Pride and Prejudice*, Miss Bingley describes her idea of an accomplished woman, as one who has '"a thorough knowledge of music, singing, drawing, dancing, and the modern languages"'. As is obvious from boarding-school prospectuses, advertisements for governesses and the specialisms of many private 'masters' or tutors, Miss Bingley wasn't alone: this really was what was

considered desirable for young women. These studies had little practical application for most people. They were also expensive to pursue. In a sense, though, that was the point.

Dancing and singing were of course conducive to flirting, but accomplishments improved a young woman's marital prospects, partly because they signalled that she came from a family that could afford to waste money. The harp lessons and the fancier types of needlework that affluent young women were also encouraged to learn: these were forms of conspicuous consumption. To have a daughter who sang songs in Italian or a wife who painted pictures was a declaration of your wealth and social status. This is why Lady Catherine de Bourgh is so bemused to discover that only two of the Bennet sisters have learned to play the piano. '"You ought all to have learned,"' she declares. '"The Miss Webbs all play, and their father has not so good an income as yours."'

It would be a mistake, however, to think that boys were necessarily better or more widely educated than their sisters. Art, music and modern languages barely got a look-in. Nor, for many boys, did science. Eton, the most famous of the elite public schools, didn't teach mathematics until 1851. Dr Thomas Arnold, headmaster of Rugby School in the 1820s and 1830s, frequently repeated his priorities for his pupils: 'First religious and moral principle, second gentlemanly conduct, third academic ability'. In the absence of any kind of school-leaving examination, getting into one of the handful of universities that then existed in the British Isles didn't always say much about someone's brains or their educational attainments. The degree choice was extremely narrow. There were several different classes of undergraduates, from those who were obliged to work their way through their degrees, perhaps even acting as servants to their fellow students, to 'gentleman-commoners', who paid a premium for extra privileges.

Some undergraduates had to study hard, win fellowships and make opportunities for themselves, like Jane's brother James and, before him, their father; some were rich enough not to need to bother with any of that. Others bypassed university altogether, going straight on to the final stage of a rich young man's education: the 'Grand Tour'. This could comprise several years spent travelling around Europe, visiting sites of historical or cultural significance in the company of a private tutor. Edward Austen really became a member of the leisured, moneyed class not when he was adopted, but when, aged eighteen, he embarked on his European tour.

Mr Collins, in *Pride and Prejudice*, may be comically dim, but he's also an Anglican clergyman and Austen makes a point of telling us that he attended 'one of the universities' – that is, either Oxford or Cambridge. We're also told that Darcy's father funded the scoundrelly George Wickham's education, enabling him to attend the University of Cambridge, but it's perfectly possible that Darcy himself didn't bother getting a degree. He doesn't, after all, need to.

In modern British culture, both boarding schools and Oxbridge are seen as aspirational, but this doesn't entirely reflect late eighteenth- and early nineteenth-century attitudes. Boarding schools ran the gamut from famous names like Eton, Harrow or Rugby to small-scale affairs with fewer than half a dozen pupils, like the one run by Jane Austen's own parents. Some cost £15 or £20 a year, and others more than twice as much. There were schools where children could receive an excellent and varied education from experienced teachers. On the other hand, if you simply wanted a child kept safely out of the way, perhaps because they were illegitimate, like Colonel Brandon's ward Eliza in *Sense and Sensibility* or Harriet Smith in *Emma* – both of whom attend boarding schools – then that could be done too.

Regulation was non-existent and neglect and abuse by teachers occasionally so shocking that it resulted in criminal convictions. One way of attempting to guard against this was to send children to schools run by relatives or acquaintances. Another was to pay a premium for them to be 'parlour boarders', receiving preferential treatment that included socializing with the headteacher and their acquaintances. This practice carried certain risks. Both families approved when Jane's sister Cassandra got engaged to a young man who had been educated by their father. But in *Sense and Sensibility*, Edward Ferrars has to keep his engagement to his tutor's niece secret because his mother has matrimonial ambitions for him. Even if there were no romantic entanglements, sending your children away meant that you were exposing them to external influences at what might be a particularly impressionable age.

Jane was first sent away to school when she was seven, and was home again for good by her eleventh birthday. The timing is unusual. Typically, parents and guardians paid boarding school fees when girls were slightly older, say from ten or twelve to about sixteen. This meant they were old enough to benefit from the specialized tuition, during the awkward adolescent phase, while not eating up too many of the years when a girl was widely considered marriageable – any age from fifteen onwards. Occasionally, though, girls stayed on at school.

Left Edward Austen, Jane Austen's brother. The portrait is thought to have been painted while he was on his Grand Tour in the late 1780s.

Below Robert Cruikshank, *Oxford Transports, or Albanians doing Penance for Past offences*, 1824. The rowdy young men are students at St Alban Hall, owned by and later absorbed into Merton College.

Schooldays

"'I would rather be teacher at a school—and I can think of nothing worse—than marry a man I did not like." "I would rather do anything than be teacher at a school," said her sister. "I have been at school, Emma, and know what a life they lead"'

The Watsons

Together with her sister Cassandra and their cousin Jane Cooper, Jane Austen attended two schools. The first was in Oxford. Jane was sent there in 1783 at the age of seven. Cassandra was then ten and Jane Cooper thirteen. The school – perhaps located in a house in Turl Street and possibly consisting just of the three of them – was run by Mrs Cawley, who, in addition to being Jane Cooper's aunt, was the widow of the Master of Brasenose College. James, the oldest of the Austen children, was then a student in Oxford, so able to check up on the girls, while their shared great-uncle, Theophilus Leigh, was still in post as the Master of Balliol College. At the time Oxford was a small city, its centre compact; they would all have been bumping into each other regularly. It sounds like a safe set-up. But at some point (so the story goes) Mrs Cawley went to Southampton, with the girls in tow. Here they took ill with typhus fever and when, after the older Jane had raised the alarm, their mothers arrived, Mrs Cooper caught the disease from them and died. Supporting evidence is fairly scant, though, so few of the details are certain.

We know more about the next school the girls attended. After spending eighteen months at home, Jane and Cassandra arrived at the Ladies Boarding School in Reading when the new term started in August 1785. Jane Cooper had already been there for a year, since her father had moved to a new parish on the outskirts of the town. The school was well-established, but after the recent death of the headmistress, it had been taken over by a junior partner: the self-styled Madame la Tournelle – in reality a former actress, Sarah Hackett, who had no educational expertise.

A much less famous author, Mary Martha Sherwood, who attended the same school in the early 1790s, wrote about it in some detail in her memoirs, published after her death by her daughter, Sophia Kelly, as *The Life of Mrs Sherwood, (chiefly Autobiographical)*. She describes a 'most ancient building, which consisted of a gateway with rooms above, and on each side of it a vast staircase', honeycombed with 'many little nooks' and 'closets' and 'many larger and smaller rooms and passages'. The best feature, she thought, was the 'beautiful old-fashioned garden, where the young ladies were allowed to wander, under tall trees, in hot summer evenings'. From Mrs Sherwood we learn that discipline was lax, and religious observance patchy – her own personal Bible being apparently 'the only Bible' she saw during her time at the school. We also learn that Madame la Tournelle was 'stout' and elderly 'but very active, though she had a cork leg'; she spoke no French, and her conversation centred on 'plays and play actors'. There were 'old novels' out on the shelves too, the kind that Mrs Sherwood's parents disapproved of.

It sounds as if in some ways it might have been quite a fruitful place for the young Jane to spend time, but she and Cassandra were removed at the end of 1786. All in all, Jane spent around two years at boarding school, costing her parents about £80 – not a trifling sum.

Above Turl Street in Oxford, possibly the location of the first school Jane attended.

Opposite Paul Sandby, detail of painting of the Ladies' Boarding School in Reading, formerly part of the old abbey, *c.*1800.

Opposite 'Europe divided into its kingdoms, etc.', by the puzzle-maker John Spilsbury, earliest known *c.*1766. A popular educational toy. In *Mansfield Park* the heroine's cousins are surprised that she '"[...] cannot put the map of Europe together [...]"'.

Harriet Smith, in *Emma*, is seventeen, and though she has been promoted from 'scholar' to 'parlour-boarder' at Mrs Goddard's school, the plan is evidently for her to remain where she is for the present. *Persuasion* mentions another seventeen-year-old girl 'still from the want of near relations and a settled home, remaining another year at school'.

The only surviving reference Austen makes to her own time away is a casual, fleeting one in a letter of 1796, addressed to her sister: 'I could die of laughter [...], as they used to say at school'. We're told in *Persuasion*, though, that Anne Elliot was deeply unhappy as a boarder, while a young girl in the short story *Lady Susan* is 'detected in an attempt to run away' from the 'academy' in which she has been enrolled by her unfeeling mother. In *Emma*, Austen explicitly criticizes the kind of fashionable 'seminary' or 'establishment [...] which professed, in long sentences of refined nonsense, to combine liberal acquirements with elegant morality [...] and where young ladies for enormous pay might be screwed out of health and into vanity'. She is less negative about the 'real, honest, old-fashioned boarding school' in Highbury, but hardly fulsome. We read that it's a place 'where a reasonable quantity of accomplishments were sold at a reasonable price, and where girls might be sent to be out of the way and scramble themselves into a little education, without any danger of coming back prodigies'.

These attitudes can be traced in a number of Austen's novels. Graduates of boarding schools include the Bingley sisters in *Pride and Prejudice*, who were 'educated at one of the first private seminaries in town' and have emerged 'proud and conceited'. There's also one very silly character in *Sense and Sensibility* who has spent 'seven years at [...] school' in London. The only 'proof' of her expensive education is a piece of embroidery, 'a landscape in coloured silks'. The Musgrove sisters, in *Persuasion*, have 'brought [...] the usual stock of accomplishments' from their school and are indistinguishable from 'thousands of other young ladies'.

Of all Austen's heroines, only one, Anne Elliot in *Persuasion*, has been sent away to school. The rest have been educated at home. Austen refers to the 'studies' of the Dashwood sisters in *Sense and Sensibility*, but these seem to be largely self-directed, and limited to the art, music and English literature that they enjoy. The youngest, Margaret, doesn't appear to have any regular lessons. Almost the only time that Elizabeth Bennet and Lady Catherine de Bourgh find themselves in agreement is in thinking that the Bennet girls have been educationally neglected. Lizzy freely admits that '"those who chose to be idle, certainly might"'. Still, even the Bennets have had access to '"all the masters that were necessary"' and Lizzy plays the piano competently, while her middle sister Mary has, we're told, progressed as far as the demanding 'thorough bass' (*basso continuo*).

By contrast, Catherine Morland, the heroine of *Northanger Abbey*, 'cannot bear' her piano lessons and is permitted to abandon them after a year. She is described at one point as having 'a very ignorant mind' – hardly surprising, given how little effort has been put into her education. Aside from the abortive piano lessons and learning to recite poems, she is taught 'writing and accounts [...] by her father' and 'French by her mother'. The rest of the time, she and her sisters are 'left to shift for themselves'. Even as a young adult, freed from homeschooling, her view remains that it is a miserable experience both for the children and the parent attempting to instruct them.

"'You think me foolish to call instruction a torment, but if you had been as much used as myself to hear poor little children first learning their letters and then learning to spell, if you had ever seen how stupid they can be for a whole morning together, and how tired my poor mother is at the end of it [...] you would allow that to torment and to instruct might sometimes be used as synonimous [sic] words'"

Northanger Abbey

Jane's governess friend

Anne Sharp is an outlier among Jane's friends. Often there were family connections or links to her father's school, or they lived in the same neighbourhood. Several were, like Jane herself, the daughters of clergymen. By contrast, Anne was employed by Jane's brother Edward as a governess and her origins remain mysterious. What records we have managed to locate suggest that she was born in London around the middle of the 1770s. Her will, written shortly before she died in 1853, mentions no relations.

We do, however, have the diary of Anne's one-time pupil, Jane's niece Fanny, and so we know quite a lot about Anne's time in Edward Austen's household. Having arrived in January 1804, she stayed for almost exactly two years. In the summer of 1805, about six months before Anne moved on, Jane and her mother and sister paid a visit to Edward at his Kent estate, Godmersham. We know that the women performed amateur dramatics with the children and we also know that in September, Jane, Cassandra and Mrs Austen went to the seaside resort of Worthing, accompanied by Edward, his wife, his eldest daughter and Anne Sharp.

Anne and Jane appear to have been drawn to each other over these months they spent together. Jane's father had passed away earlier in the year and a few weeks before that, her old friend Anne Lefroy had died after a riding accident; it was probably an emotionally fraught period in her life, when friendship was particularly appreciated. There are tantalizing links between Anne Sharp and Jane's novels: the theatricals which take place in *Mansfield Park*; the heroine's governess in *Emma*, whose first name is Anne; *Persuasion*, where another Anne visits the seaside. As is often the case with Jane, speculation has bloomed in all kinds of directions, but the two appear to have seen little of each other after 1805, and references to Anne in Jane's letters are not always entirely kind. In one, Jane calls Anne 'poor thing'; another indicates impatience with Anne's enthusiasm for quack doctors. However, Jane attempted – though seemingly failed – to arrange for Anne to come to Chawton in 1811, and there was a brief visit in 1815. What's more significant, perhaps, is that Anne was sent a presentation copy of *Emma*. One of Jane's last letters was written to Anne, who felt that the relationship had been sufficiently close to merit requesting a lock of hair after her friend died. With it, Cassandra decided to send some small personal mementoes: 'a pair of clasps which she sometimes wore & a small bodkin [presumably a sewing implement] which she had had in constant use for more than twenty years'.

Anne continued to pursue a career in education, at length setting up a school near Liverpool. According to the notice of her death, she was 'mourned by a large circle of friends', a claim borne out by her will, in which she bequeathed money, jewellery and ornaments to many people, one a goddaughter. It's evident that she did well for herself.

Running your own school was widely considered preferable to working as a governess. All private tutors had a difficult line to tread, but there were additional challenges facing governesses. Since you were required to be both ladylike and accomplished, the fact that you were now obliged to work for your living usually meant there was some misfortune behind you – bereavement or financial losses. You were socially inferior to the family, but at the same time superior to the other servants and would thus find it difficult to make friends. You had to remain on good terms with your employers and their guests, but without risking over-familiarity. Often governesses were vulnerable to sexual harassment or assault. In *Emma*, Anne Taylor has been treated more like a sister than a governess, and in that she's been extraordinarily lucky. Jane Fairfax – rightly – dreads embarking on the same career.

Right Fanny Austen-Knight, the niece of Cassandra and Jane Austen

Below R. Page, *Hester Chapone*, c.1812. Chapone had actually died over a decade before this picture was produced but her work remained influential into the nineteenth century.

Lady Catherine puts great faith in governesses and their ability to provide '"steady and regular instruction"' but – as Austen suggests – they varied just as much as schools did. There's a governess in the short fiction *Lady Susan* who appears to have taught her young charge almost nothing. Emma's governess Miss Taylor is an 'excellent woman' with 'powers' (that is, abilities, skills) but the 'mildness of her temper' made her, it's clear, a fairly ineffectual teacher. Though naturally bright, Emma has been permitted to waste years in 'idleness' and according to the critical but not unjust Mr Knightley, has learned neither '"industry"' nor '"patience"'. More professional is Miss Lee, the governess at *Mansfield Park*, who runs a disciplined schoolroom and manages to instil a good deal of information into the heads of her pupils. Miss Lee doesn't just provide lessons in the standard French, art and music; she listens to each girl read a 'portion of history' daily, teaches them geography and a sprinkling of classics and philosophy, and even touches on chemistry. There's a fair amount of reading aloud and rote learning, which Austen appears critical of, but neither were unusual teaching techniques at the time. The syllabus is a good one and includes the latest teaching aids, such as jigsaw-puzzle maps of Europe to be 'put together'. There are even informal examinations when Miss Lee's employer, Sir Thomas Bertram, checks how his daughters and niece are progressing in their studies.

It's disappointing that Austen doesn't show more interest in the character of Miss Lee, especially given that she had by this point become friendly with Anne Sharp, her niece Fanny's governess. And it's strange that she's not more positive about the effects of what, by the standards of the early nineteenth century, is a thorough, well-balanced education.

The Bertram girls turn out to be 'entirely deficient in [...] self-knowledge, generosity, and humility'. Their 'anxious and expensive education' has 'no useful influence [...] no moral effect upon the mind' – or so their disappointed father concludes, when one commits adultery and the other elopes. A similar idea appears, slightly softened, in *Emma*, where Jane Fairfax – probably the most highly educated female character in Austen's fiction – enters into an ill-advised secret engagement.

Opposite Charles Escot, *Jean-Jacques Rousseau*, 1874. Rousseau's unorthodox ideas on education were enormously influential in the late eighteenth century.

There are perhaps traces of sour grapes here, because Austen's own education is best described as haphazard. But she was not the only writer to argue that fashionable schools and expensive private tutors often failed to impart the most important lessons. Like so many issues during Jane's lifetime, education was politicized and hotly debated.

Take the influential Swiss philosopher Jean-Jacques Rousseau, whose ideas were closely followed by a number of British families. Disapproving of formal schooling, he was all for fresh air and exercise and learning by observation, though he managed to square this with the idea that girls should be taught the accomplishments that would entertain their husbands. In *A Vindication of the Rights of Woman*, Mary Wollstonecraft wrote dismissively of the pointless 'smattering of accomplishments' that was usually insisted on. Instead, she advocated for science experiments, lessons in modern and classical languages and co-ed schooling. The writer Hester Chapone suggested in *Letters on the Improvement of the Mind* that accomplishments were valuable, though less to attract suitors or entertain husbands than for what they offered young women: interest, pleasure, a chance to gain skills and achieve something for themselves. She also thought it important for girls to be taught how to manage a household competently, especially accounts – an area, she suggested, 'too often wholly neglected in a young woman's education'.

But still more important for Chapone than managing servants or a solid grounding in arithmetic was 'reading, well chosen and properly regulated', which she argued ought to be considered 'chief' among the 'accomplishments'. Austen seems to have agreed with her. Famously, Darcy says that while of course an accomplished woman will be able to sing and draw and dance and speak modern foreign languages, she should also '"add something more substantial, in the improvement of her mind by extensive reading"'. Chapone is also echoed by Edmund Bertram in *Mansfield Park*, who, by recommending books to his cousin, 'assist[s] the improvement of her mind'. 'A fondness for reading' is, Austen suggests in that novel, 'an education in itself' if 'properly directed'. Most of her heroines haven't received much schooling, but they are almost all readers.

As the eighteenth century drew to a close, there was a lot to read. More books and newspapers and magazines were being printed than ever before: children's books and text books and cookery books, novels, histories, translations, volumes of poetry, treatises on art and agriculture, literary reviews and publications aimed specifically at women. Most remained expensive to buy, but the spread of circulating libraries was starting to bring a wide range of texts within the reach of anyone who could afford a subscription. Book and newspaper clubs, where a number of individuals pooled their money together, extended access even further. There was a thriving market in second-hand books and in cheap short-form publications like pamphlets, ballads and broadsheets, which were brought even to out-of-the-way places by travelling salesmen. Chapbooks – cheap, poorly illustrated and indifferently written folktales and fiction – had been around for more than a century. Suddenly, alongside them appeared political texts: condensed editions of Thomas Paine's *Rights of Man*, for example, and, from the opposing camp, the *Cheap Repository Tracts*, conservative propaganda in the form of readily affordable (or even free) reading material.

'She never could learn or understand anything before she was taught; and sometimes not even then, for she was often inattentive, and occasionally stupid. Her mother was three months in teaching her only to repeat the "Beggar's Petition"; and after all, her next sister, Sally, could say it better than she did. Not that Catherine was always stupid—by no means; she learnt the fable of "The Hare and Many Friends" as quickly as any girl in England. Her mother wished her to learn music; and Catherine was sure she should like it, for she was very fond of tinkling the keys of the old forlorn spinnet; so, at eight years old she began. She learnt a year, and could not bear it; and Mrs. Morland, who did not insist on her daughters being accomplished in spite of incapacity or distaste, allowed her to leave off. [...] Her taste for drawing was not superior; though whenever she could obtain the outside of a letter from her mother or seize upon any other odd piece of paper, she did what she could in that way, by drawing houses and trees, hens and chickens, all very much like one another. Writing and accounts she was taught by her father; French by her mother: her proficiency in either was not remarkable, and she shirked her lessons in both whenever she could.'

Northanger Abbey

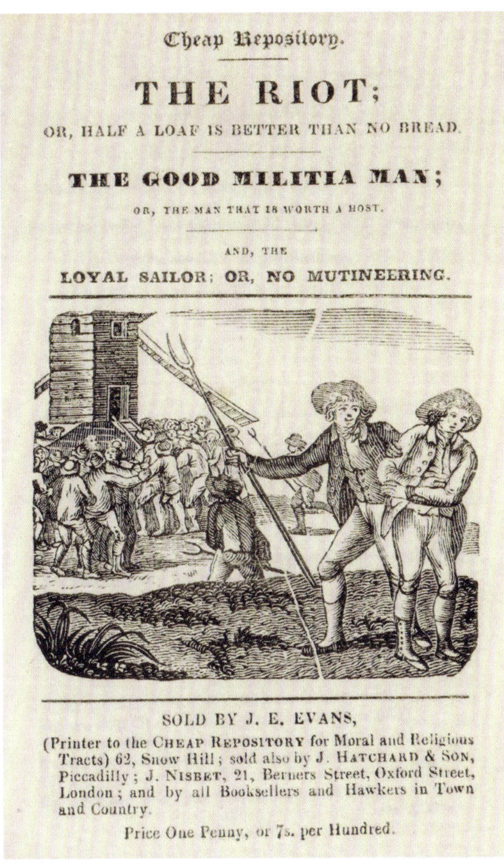

Cheap Repository.

THE RIOT;

OR, HALF A LOAF IS BETTER THAN NO BREAD.

THE GOOD MILITIA MAN;

OR, THE MAN THAT IS WORTH A HOST.

AND, THE

LOYAL SAILOR; OR, NO MUTINEERING.

SOLD BY J. E. EVANS,

(Printer to the CHEAP REPOSITORY for Moral and Religious Tracts) 62, Snow Hill; sold also by J. HATCHARD & SON, Piccadilly; J. NISBET, 21, Berners Street, Oxford Street, London; and by all Booksellers and Hawkers in Town and Country.

Price One Penny, or 7s. per Hundred.

Left The title page of *The Riot or Half a loaf is better than no bread*, first circulated in the second half of the 1790s. This is one of the conservative Cheap Repository Tracts aimed at the working classes.

Below After John Downman, *Richmal Mangnall*, early 19th century. Mangnall's text-book was used in many schools and homes.

Though formal schooling was inaccessible to many, and even for those who were lucky enough to get it, often limited to a small number of subjects, the written word offered infinite possibilities.

Books could teach you almost anything.
An upwardly mobile tradesman could learn the conventions and shibboleths of upper-class behaviour from one of the many 'conduct books' available, and find ones aimed at his children, too. A harassed housewife could hand her sulky daughter a moral essay to read, just like Catherine Morland's mother does towards the end of *Northanger Abbey*. A well-meaning aunt could buy her niece French books designed for children, like *Fables Choisies* or *L'ami de l'adolescence* (The Friend of Youth): and in fact Jane's aunt Philadelphia appears to have bought her both of these texts. There were also books that were both conduct literature and teaching material, such as *Mentoria, Or, the Young Ladies Instructor*, first published in 1778, a copy of which was in the Austen household. Written by a woman called Ann Murry, a well-regarded teacher who counted the Princess Royal among her pupils, this consists of a series of dialogues between a governess, Mentoria, and her pupils, taking in subjects as diverse as the 'duties of life', the 'rudiments of geography' and the 'Spartan form of government'. Dialogue 9 contains 'a brief Explanation of Grammar, Logic, Rhetoric, Arithmetic, Geometry, Astronomy, and Music' – very brief, since the chapter is only twenty-five pages long.

The turn of the century saw the arrival of a similar but more ambitious text written by another female teacher, Richmal Mangnall's *Historical and Miscellaneous Questions*.

Below Daniel Nikolaus Chodowiecki, two illustrations for Samuel Richardson's *Clarissa*, 1785. Richardson's novels remained popular and widely read into Austen's adulthood.

'our family [...] are great Novel-readers & not ashamed of being so'

Letter from Jane Austen to her sister, 18-19 December 1798

This included lots of British and European history 'from the early age' onwards, a list of Latin phrases, the 'elements of astronomy', 'mineralogy' and metallurgy and a host of other facts. It's actually quite informative. It may also be the book that inspired the education that the Bertram girls and their cousin Fanny receive in *Mansfield Park*; there are distinct overlaps. Mangnall's *Questions* sold in vast numbers through the nineteenth century and is mentioned by name in numerous Victorian novels. Though the references are often mocking, it must have influenced and informed thousands upon thousands of young minds, as well as inculcating a habit of asking questions.

Culture was made accessible too, in the form of miscellanies like the *Elegant Extracts*, which collected what were considered the best passages of poetry and prose. In *Northanger Abbey*, Austen expresses impatience that 'the man who collects and publishes in a volume some dozen lines of Milton, Pope, and Prior, with a paper from the Spectator, and a chapter from Sterne' should be praised, while 'novel writers' are criticized. Elsewhere she is less negative about miscellanies. In *Emma*, the young farmer Robert Martin may reserve most of his reading time for the 'Agricultural Reports', but the family also owns 'the Elegant Extracts' and we're told he reads aloud from it in the evenings. In the process, he's picked up a decent writing style; Emma is taken aback when she discovers how well the letter in which he proposes to her friend Harriet is composed. Austen's niece Anna owned a copy of the prose *Elegant Extracts*, inscribed as 'the gift of her Aunt Jane'.

In the first chapter of *Northanger Abbey*, Austen details how the heroine Catherine's tomboyish girlhood gives way, once she is fifteen and 'in training for a heroine', to reading poetry and drama. Jane Austen, we know, read both too, but – being in training for a novelist, rather than a heroine – she also read novels.

Prose fiction was viewed with a measure of distrust, in part, it seems, precisely because young people tended to enjoy it. Fordyce suggested in his *Sermons* that few novels could be read 'with safety' by young women, 'and yet fewer [...] with advantage'. The only novel he recommended, somewhat strangely to modern thinking, is Samuel Richardson's *Clarissa, Or, The History of a Young Lady*, a vast and very popular work published in 1748, which features abusive parenting, attempted seduction, anorexia and rape. Richardson was also the author of *Pamela* and *Sir Charles Grandison*, the former of which concerns a man's obsession with his mother's maidservant and contains many sexually explicit passages. Wollstonecraft, who is otherwise almost entirely opposed to Fordyce's thinking, agrees with him in considering fiction undesirable, filled with 'unnatural and meretricious scenes'. She suggests it's necessary to 'correct' a 'fondness for novels'. Other writers on education were, though cautious, more positive. Rousseau enthusiastically recommended Defoe's *Robinson Crusoe* for young boys, while Chapone admitted that there were novels 'in which excellent morality is joined with the most lively pictures of the human mind that can entertain the imagination and interest the heart'.

There is a short biographical essay, usually attributed to Henry Austen, which was published with *Persuasion* and *Northanger Abbey* shortly after Jane died. It claims that her favourite novel was Richardson's *Sir Charles Grandison* – the story of an exemplary man torn romantically between two very different women. We do have the manuscript of a five-act play, a short dramatic adaptation of *Sir Charles Grandison* in what seems to be

Opposite Maria Edgeworth, after Alonzo Chappel, c.1873.

Austen's handwriting, so we're safe in saying she was familiar with his work. The essay is also definite about Jane's 'favourite moral writers' – Samuel Johnson and the poet William Cowper. All the authors referred to are, you may notice, men. But we know from other sources that Austen also admired female writers, and not just people like Chapone and Wollstonecraft, but novelists as well, many of whom published under their own names.

The likes of Ann Radcliffe and Charlotte Smith, and even Frances Burney and Maria Edgeworth, are seldom read nowadays. But they outsold Jane Austen by significant margins and were once far better known than she was. Ann Radcliffe was the author of Gothic novels – lurid tales where young heroines face mysterious and possibly supernatural dangers in atmospheric settings. These enjoyed a considerable vogue in the last quarter of the eighteenth century. *The Mysteries of Udolpho*, which Catherine Morland reads in *Northanger Abbey*, was by Radcliffe, and so was *The Romance of the Forest*, which is mentioned in *Emma*. Saddled with a profligate, unreliable husband, Charlotte Smith wrote to maintain herself and her children, producing ten novels as well as children's books and poetry. If you were to read her *Emmeline, The Orphan of the Castle*, you might be strongly reminded, once or twice, of *Persuasion*. We know that Austen first encountered the novel when she was a teenager, because she mentions a character from it in her own *History of England*. She must also have been familiar with Smith's *Celestina*, which anticipates *Sense and Sensibility* in several points, even down to having a character named Willoughby who suddenly and inexplicably abandons the heroine. The echoes are intentional and meant to be recognized by readers.

When, in 1797, Jane's father sent off one of her manuscripts to a publisher, he described it as being 'about the length of Miss Burney's Evelina'. *Evelina* was an epistolary novel which appeared anonymously in 1778 and met with such success that the identity of its author was soon discovered and made public. Burney became famous and, in between embarking on a career at court, and the years she spent trapped in France with her French husband after the brief Peace of Amiens was broken in 1803, she wrote three other novels: *Cecilia* in 1782, *Camilla* in 1796 and *The Wanderer* in 1814.

'Miss J Austen, Steventon' is listed as one of the subscribers to *Camilla*; it is one of the few times that Austen's name appeared in print during her lifetime, never associated with her own work. Subscriptions were then a common form of crowdfunding, but the cost – a guinea – represented a substantial amount of money to Jane and presumably she must have been a fan. It is possible that she got the title *Pride and Prejudice* from the conclusion of *Cecilia*, where it's mentioned several times in the space of a paragraph, though it was, as has been mentioned before, a phrase used fairly widely. In *Northanger Abbey* the absurd John Thorpe manages to both praise Burney and criticize her under her married name of D'Arblay, apparently unaware that he's talking about the same woman. At one point Austen breaks off the story to mount an impassioned defence of her chosen genre, naming 'Cecilia, or Camilla, or Belinda' (the last of which was written by Maria Edgeworth) as prime examples of the novel, books 'in which the greatest powers of the mind are displayed, in which the most thorough knowledge of human nature, the happiest delineation of its varieties, the liveliest effusions of wit and humour are conveyed to the world in the best chosen language'.

'My uncle's barn is fitting up quite like a theatre, & all the young folks are to take their part'

Letter written by Jane's cousin, Phila Walter, describing the preparations for amateur theatricals at Steventon

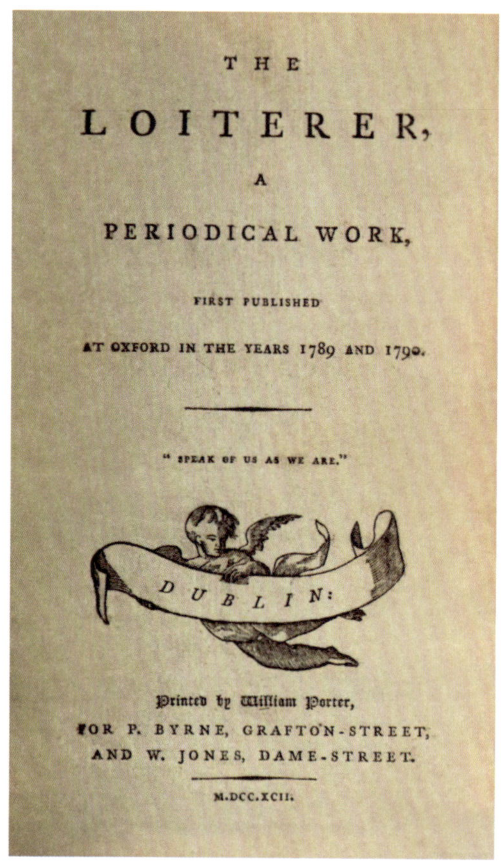
THE

LOITERER,

A

PERIODICAL WORK,

FIRST PUBLISHED

AT OXFORD IN THE YEARS 1789 AND 1790.

"SPEAK OF US AS WE ARE."

DUBLIN:

Printed by William Porter,

FOR P. BYRNE, GRAFTON-STREET,

AND W. JONES, DAME-STREET.

M.DCC.XCII.

Below *The Loiterer*, the magazine produced and edited by Jane Austen's brothers while they were at Oxford.

Despite this extravagant praise, Burney is unlikely to prove particularly engaging for modern readers. She paints with a broader brush than Austen. Her plots are melodramatic and highly improbable, her characters stock ones: the beautiful and innocent heroine, the evil baronet, the crass and embarrassing relatives who make their living by trade. There may be method in Austen's enthusiasm, though; several of the dark arts of book promotion had already been invented by the end of the eighteenth century. When *Emma* was published, a complimentary copy was sent to the successful Anglo-Irish author Maria Edgeworth, though she was underwhelmed, complaining in a letter written to her brother in 1816 that there was 'no story in it'.

But Austen had in fact learned a lot from her. Edgeworth's father owned an estate in Ireland called Edgeworthstown (there's still a town of that name, also called Mostrim). He was, however, linked to the largely liberal Birmingham-based Lunar Society, and unlike many Anglo-Irish landowning families, the Edgeworths were not 'absentees'. Rather than living in England and drawing income from the estate, they instead made their home there. They were interested in Irish culture and sympathetic to calls for Catholic emancipation. During the United Irish Uprising of 1798, they were suspected of conspiring with the rebels and their connection with the well-known radical publisher Joseph Johnson didn't counter lingering concerns over their politics. Nor did Maria's book *Castle Rackrent*, published in 1800. This told the story of one Irish estate and several generations of its owners; by no stretch of the imagination could it be read as a straightforward endorsement of what had been happening in Ireland over the past century. The following year Maria published a novel, *Belinda*, ostensibly about a young woman navigating the perils of fashionable society as she looks for a husband, but really concerned with attitudes to women and, to a lesser degree, race. Edgeworth demonstrated that women could write about political and social issues, but her career also showed how those issues might be made more palatable to the public by being blended with comedy and romance.

Anne Lefroy

It's difficult to know how best to describe the woman who is often referred to as 'Madame' or 'Madam' Lefroy. For a start, she wasn't French. She was born Anne Brydges, in Kent, and while her husband's family did have French roots, they'd been living in the British Isles – and before that in the trading centre of Leghorn or Livorno, in Italy – for decades. She was a long-term neighbour of the Austens, residing near Steventon in the village of Ashe, where her husband was vicar. She was under the impression that she was also a connection, a distant cousin of Mrs Austen, with both their families claiming descent from the Brydges, who held the title of Baron Chandos. When Mrs Lefroy's brother attempted to assert his claim to the title, however, he was, after much litigation, rejected, being unable to prove the link.

Anne Lefroy was, by marriage, Tom Lefroy's aunt, and it's not implausible that characters like Mrs Gardiner in *Pride and Prejudice* and Lady Russell in *Persuasion* – sensible older women who advise caution in love – might be partly modelled on her. But while we're uncertain what Jane felt about Tom or whether their relationship ever actually amounted to anything significant, we can speak with greater confidence about her relationship with Anne.

Though old enough to have been Jane's mother, Mrs Lefroy was quite a lot younger than Mrs Austen. She ran a daily school in her own home, where she taught local children to read and write. She set up a small business to offer employment. She administered hundreds of smallpox vaccinations with her own hands. She also found time to take an interest in Jane – something which may have been crucial to the younger woman's intellectual and artistic development. It's believed that Mrs Lefroy had succeeded in having verse and prose pieces published, and she had the reputation of being both extremely clever and a gifted writer.

A lengthy obituary notice which appeared in the *Kentish Weekly Post* shortly after her death claims that: 'Nature had endowed her with powers of intellect very rare, with a rapidity of perception, an extent of comprehension, and a command of [...] language, which from her childhood drew forth wonder and applause; her talents for Poetry displayd [sic] themselves before she was 12 years old, and various were her compositions in early life'

In December 1804 Anne Lefroy fell from her horse, dying half a day later – on Saturday 16, which was Jane's twenty-ninth birthday. In a poem entitled 'To the Memory of Mrs Lefroy' and preserved among her papers, Jane calls her 'Beloved friend', talks of her 'Talents', her 'Eloquence', her 'smile benign' and 'Her partial favour from my earliest years'. She suggests that the coincidence of dates indicates a link between them and expresses the wish that she might meet Anne in heaven one day. Clearly, the friendship meant a great deal to her.

Above Portrait miniature of Anne Lefroy, probably Richard Crosse, 1780. Anne Lefroy was Austen's friend and possibly her literary mentor too.

"'Let us be doing something. Be it only half a play, an act, a scene; what should prevent us?'"

Mansfield Park

Opposite Eliza Austen, née Hancock, later 'Comtesse' de Feuillide, as a young girl. Austen's cousin and sister-in-law.

There were other writers Jane learned from, too. Several members of her family fancied themselves as poets or essayists. We have a number of her mother's verses. James, the eldest of the Austen children, also wrote poetry and when he and Henry were at university, they ran their own magazine called *The Loiterer.* Jane would have read (or heard) letters written by friends and family. In a household where most of the occupants were studying Greek and Latin literature almost daily, she must have picked up something. She would have regularly listened to sermons in church which, because of the educational system vicars had been put through, also tended to be strongly influenced by classical rhetoric. Her cousin Edward Cooper published his sermons. Another cousin, Cassandra Cooke, also made it into print, with a novel called *Battleridge*, which appeared anonymously in 1801. Then there's Anne Lefroy, who, in spite of the age difference between them, seems to have taken on the role of a mentor to Jane.

While we shouldn't necessarily believe the family's claim, in the early biographical essay, that Jane remained 'submissive to criticism' of her more mature work, there were people around her, especially when she was younger, whose feedback and encouragement may have proved invaluable.

Plays provided lessons too. Trips to the theatre were only ever a very occasional treat for the Austens, but the family took amateur dramatics seriously. The barn at Steventon was turned into a theatre, with reusable sets. Jane's older brothers composed prologues and epilogues for their performances and Jane herself penned two brief comedies, *The Visit* and *The Mystery.* These seem to be early works, belonging to about 1789, when Jane would have been thirteen, but they feature lists of *dramatis personae* and stage directions. We're not sure whether they were performed, however.

One work we know the 'young folks' at the rectory did put on was *The Chances*, based on one of those seventeenth-century plays where a series of unlikely misunderstandings and coincidences ends by tying all the characters together in one large complicated knot. Another was *The Wonder: A Woman Keeps a Secret*, written in the early eighteenth century by the dramatist Susannah Centlivre, whose work enjoyed considerable popularity during Jane's lifetime. They also performed pieces like *Tom Thumb, Bon Ton or High Life Above Stairs* and the farce *The Sultan, or A Peep into the Seraglio.* In this last, which has, unsurprisingly, dated quite badly, Jane's cousin Jane Cooper took the central role of the witty, argumentative Roxalana, who, though she causes havoc, succeeds in winning the heart and hand of the sultan, played by Henry Austen. Both were in their late teens. The Austens' older and far more glamorous cousin, Eliza, also took part in some of the plays. She was at this point married to a Frenchman and used the title of Comtesse de Feuillide. She eventually married Henry Austen, though, and James Austen is also supposed to have been one of her admirers.

Good dialogue was one thing Jane probably took from these performances. Even in her early work many of her characters speak quite naturally, especially when compared to other fiction from the period, and it's noticeable that screenwriters have rarely felt the need to alter much of what she gives people to say. But she may well also have observed. Given her age, it's unlikely that she had large parts and so, like Fanny Price during the play rehearsals which take up several chapters in *Mansfield Park*, she would have had plenty of opportunity to watch the rest of the cast interacting with each other, to glimpse flirtations, disagreements and jealousies.

There were things she never did learn, however. In the manuscript of *Sanditon*, produced when Jane was in her

Cousin Eliza

Betsy, Eliza, the Comtesse de Feuillide, Mrs Henry Austen: call her what you will, Eliza Austen, *née* Hancock, was a dazzling personality. The daughter of Jane's Aunt Philadelphia, Eliza was born in India, raised there and, afterwards, in England, with every advantage. She received a fortune from her godfather. In France she was courted by a handsome, titled military officer and married him. The marriage proved a disappointment to both of them, since her fortune was smaller than he had imagined and his title was self-bestowed. His real support for the opponents of the revolution was, however, enough to get him guillotined in 1794. Eliza, who had already taken refuge in England, learned of his death – and the manner of it – from a news report. A few years earlier she had nursed her mother through breast cancer, which proved fatal. Her only child, a son called Hastings, had developmental delay, probably caused by cerebral palsy. We know that she became close to her employee Madame Bigeon, and to Madame Bigeon's daughter, suggesting gratitude but perhaps also loneliness.

Her second marriage, in 1797, to her cousin, Jane's brother Henry, must have looked like a safe option that would keep her, her money and her son far better protected than they otherwise would have been. In the event, Hastings died during his teens. She herself suffered a lingering illness before her death at the age of fifty-one, in 1813, just a few years before Henry's bank collapsed, leaving him owing thousands.

In spite of unhappiness, Eliza's life was much more glamorous than Jane's was. She loved parties and flirting, and moved in elite social circles in both France and Britain. She has often been identified as the inspiration for Jane's worldlier characters, such as the man-eating Lady Susan or the fashionable Mary Crawford. She also shows, though, how cruel Jane's world sometimes was, and how money didn't always offer much protection, especially to women.

early forties, we find her using spellings like 'beleive' and 'Travellor'. Capitalization is random. She misses out possessive apostrophes. Her punctuation is eccentric. In the first edition of *Emma* the objectionable Mrs Elton used an Italian phrase which appears to be grammatically wrong. It may have been a printer's error. If not, though, it's unclear whether the mistake belongs to the character or to her creator. In fact, though Jane appears to have been reasonably proficient so far as music goes, and Cassandra to have been a competent artist – at least when she was copying other pictures – it's doubtful whether either of the Austen sisters would have been deemed accomplished by, say, someone like Miss Bingley.

Jane received a disjointed education, with myriad different and sometimes contradictory influences, and like many of her contemporaries, and nearly all her main characters, she found on reaching adulthood that she still had a good deal left to learn.

City

'Here I am in this Scene of Dissipation & vice, and I begin already to find my Morals corrupted'

Letter from Jane Austen to her sister Cassandra

For much of her life, London was somewhere Jane visited when she was en route somewhere else, or to stay with her brother Henry and his wife, Cousin Eliza. She had fun there. In a letter written to Cassandra in 1796 she laughingly calls it 'this Scene of Dissipation & vice' and jokes that she 'begin[s] already to find my Morals corrupted'. She liked the theatres and Astley's, an early circus, and entertained herself at art exhibitions by finding portraits which matched her idea of her characters (in another letter of May 1813 she says she was 'very well pleased [...] with a small picture of Mrs Bingley [i.e. Jane Bennet from *Pride and Prejudice*], excessively like her').

It is clear that she knew the city fairly well, because she always places her characters in the addresses that they'd have been likely to occupy. The Bennet girls' tradesman uncle, for example, lives in Gracechurch Street in the City of London, near the docks, while in *Sense and Sensibility* the Dashwood sisters go shopping in Bond Street. Several quite important events in the novels take place in London, but that's usually off-screen. The exception is *Sense and Sensibility*, roughly a third of which is set there, though without giving much sense of the place. As Jane's career began to progress, she did spend more time in London on business, but the capital doesn't seem to have stirred her creatively in the way other locations did. The city of Bath, however, proved a particularly rich source of inspiration.

Bath is famous now, at least in part, because of its association with Jane Austen but in her time it was famous chiefly as a health resort and social destination. The city lies at the bottom of a steep-sided valley, surrounded by limestone hills through which the rain filters to feed several hot springs. These have been attracting visitors for millennia. Legend claims that King Bladud founded a settlement there about 800 BC,

Opposite Thomas Rowlandson, *Astley's Amphitheatre*, 1808, after Auguste Charles Pugin. Austen visited Astley's in 1796 and it is mentioned in *Emma*.

Publishers

Austen's relationships with her first two publishers were carried out at several removes. We think that her brother Henry found both of them for her. The initial negotiations with Crosby & Co. concerning *Susan* were made by a Mr Seymour, possibly William Seymour, a legal acquaintance of Henry's. With his background in the militia, Henry is also the obvious likely link to Thomas Egerton, who published *Sense and Sensibility*, *Pride and Prejudice* and *Mansfield Park*. Egerton's list consisted mostly of military books, with a smattering of medical, political and educational titles, and he wasn't an obvious choice to publish a novel. While he didn't treat Jane as cavalierly as Crosby had, he was hard-headed enough to buy the copyright for *Pride and Prejudice* for £110 (about £6,500 in today's money) and over time she grew dissatisfied with him. His edition of *Mansfield Park*, which was ridden with printing errors, may have proved the final straw.

For her fourth novel, *Emma*, published at the end of 1815, Jane moved from Egerton to John Murray, a considerable step up. Murray published Lord Byron and Robert Southey, by this point Poet Laureate. He produced a magazine, *The Quarterly Review*. He had a wide literary acquaintance, including people like Sir Walter Scott.

In a letter of October 1815, Jane identified him as 'a Rogue, of course, but a civil one' but, Henry being at that time unwell, she corresponded with him herself. In fact on this occasion she stayed in London for several months, looking after her brother, attempting to keep Murray to the agreed timetable and, later, correcting proof sheets of the new novel. She was visited by the Prince Regent's librarian, James Stanier Clarke, and invited to Carlton House, which, since George III was again unwell, was effectively the main royal court. There she was informed by Clarke that she might, if she chose, dedicate her next novel to the prince, as, after consulting with Murray, she duly did.

It's an intriguing insight into Austen's growing professionalism; rather than sitting in a retired cottage, we see her at the centre of a busy London literary scene.

Below Rudolph Ackermann, *View of the exterior entrance to Carlton House*, 1809. Carlton House was the London residence of the Prince Regent.

after curing his leprosy by following the example of some pigs who wallowed in the warm mud. Legend also claims, mind you, that he was a magician and necromancer who died while attempting to fly. Still, archaeological finds suggest that Britons had been in the area long before the Romans arrived and built a city they named Aquae Sulis ('The Waters of Sulis') after a local goddess.

If the waters did drop out of use after the Romans left, it wasn't for long. Hospitals were built in the mediaeval period and dedicated bathing facilities maintained. Kings and queens visited. By the beginning of the eighteenth century, the city was well on the way to becoming fashionable. Spas were the order of the day and there were others – Tunbridge Wells, the Hotwells at Bristol, Buxton, Malvern, Cheltenham, Harrogate and elsewhere – but Bath reigned supreme. In part this was due to the influence of Beau Nash, the first semi-official master of ceremonies, and in part to the mild climate and excellent transport connections. There were also several large-scale building projects, which created the attractive, architecturally cohesive Georgian city centre that would have been familiar to Austen. In spite of the bombs that fell during the Second World War, much about the city would be familiar to her still. It's one of the best places to follow in the footsteps of the author and her characters.

Above Thomas Rowlandson, *Bath Races*, 1810. Bath was a favourite resort for invalids in spite of its steep hills.

Georgian spa days

Before bathing, it was considered necessary (according to the *New Bath Guide*) that 'the blood-vessels should not be too full' and that the stomach and bowels should be 'cleansed'. You would find a surgeon to bleed you, if that was deemed necessary, probably using one of the terrifying-looking instruments designed for the purpose. You would also take some form of laxative. Then, any time from 6.30 a.m. onwards, and before you'd had breakfast, you would take yourself to one of the baths, where an attendant would help you to change and immerse yourself. Bathing over, you would get dressed again and go to the Pump Room to *drink* the waters, unless you'd had some brought to you while you were in the bath.

There was also the option of the quieter Hetling Pump Room to drink in, but the larger, newer one was the place to be seen and would have been getting full from about 7.30 or 8 a.m. Even those who weren't bathing and had no health concerns would occasionally take a glass or two, while those who were sickly were prescribed at least a pint a day, and sometimes as much as four pints (more than two litres). As you drank, you would walk about the room, chatting to your acquaintance. At 10.30 a.m. it was time for a late breakfast, followed by some form of gentle exercise, such as walking or going for a drive. You could also receive other therapies – Edward Austen tried 'Electricity', which was recommended for gouty symptoms.

Later on you might return to the Pump Room for what Austen, in one letter written to Cassandra in May 1801, calls 'the second glass' and take another stroll. Around the middle of the afternoon it would be time to start thinking about dinner. Affluent Georgians didn't really do lunch, since even in fashionable circles, the main meal of the day began not long after 6 p.m. and it remained usual for it to take place a good couple of hours earlier than that. There would be plenty of time left in the evening still, so that you could visit the theatre or the assembly rooms, where you might dance or play cards as the fancy took you. Bath kept early hours in comparison with London, with dances finishing at 11 p.m. sharp, ready for a good night's sleep.

Below William Blackamore, *A perspective view of the old rooms, part of the Abbey, the walks and part of the park*, c.1785.

‘Every morning now brought its regular duties—shops were to be visited; some new part of the town to be looked at; and the Pump-room to be attended, where they paraded up and down for an hour’

Northanger Abbey

The Bath springs are hot – 45°C (113°F) when they emerge from the ground – and high in minerals. The water quality is monitored nowadays, so drinking it won't do you any harm, even though it tastes like warm copper coins, and immersing yourself in it probably is fairly beneficial to your muscles and joints. During Jane's lifetime, though, medicine was still very much developing and the dividing lines between medical and complementary therapies were not clear. Many illnesses and health conditions were poorly understood and there was often little that could be done, hence the popularity of ointments and tinctures, and the tendency of medical men to prescribe trips to seaside resorts and spa towns.

Though those with ‘haemorrhages, inflammations, or bad lungs’ were advised to steer clear, the *New Bath Guide*, published in 1791, suggests that the waters were considered helpful ‘in almost all chronical distempers’, particularly gout, rheumatism, paralysis, ‘bilious colick’ (bowel and stomach problems), ‘obstructions of the liver and spleen, jaundice, scurvy, loss of appetite, and hysterick and hypochondriack disorders’ [sic]. That covered a lot of people, and since most spa regimes recommended several weeks of drinking and bathing, they formed a captive market. An entire economy sprang up to service their needs, to entertain them and sell to them and their families.

The guidebook includes lists of lodgings, of doctors, surgeons, apothecaries and ‘chymists’, but also of portrait artists. It states the standard charges for the chairmen who would take you around the city in sedan chairs – covered boxes which held one person, carried about on poles. It mentions nearby tourist attractions and other resorts that people might like to move on to. And it details the well-organized leisure activities that were available in the city. In the Pump Room, where

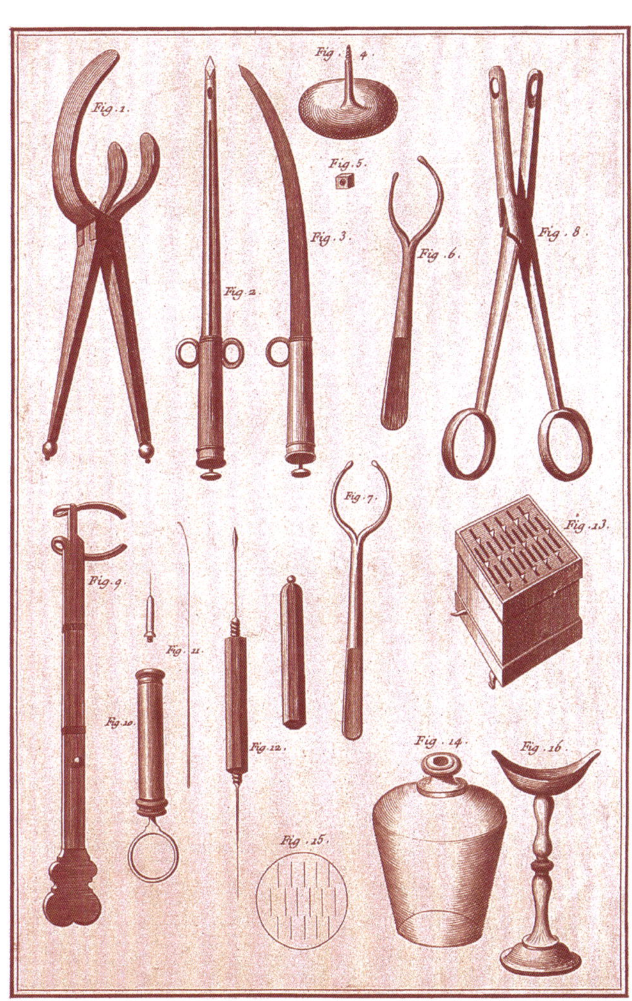

Above Several of these instruments were designed specifically for ‘bleeding’, a common pseudo-medical procedure.

Below 'Fashionable Walking Dresses in December 1807', from *La Belle Assemblée* or *Bell's Court and Fashionable Magazine*, 1808.

people collected early in the day to drink the water, there was live music. There were two assembly rooms – the 'lower', on the flat ground by the river, and the 'upper', a little way uphill. Each offered two evening balls a week, carefully arranged on different days, and card playing. The theatre opened on Tuesdays, Thursdays and Saturdays. On Wednesday evening there were concerts. The pleasure gardens hosted public breakfasts and teas, with music and regular 'illuminations, fire-works and entertainments'. You could learn to ride, and men could play tennis. There were coffee houses, where men could read the newspapers and talk politics, and libraries, open to anyone who could pay the relatively small subscription. And there were shops.

Clothes mattered in Bath, where visitors and locals alike spent so much of their time on public display, both indoors and out. You needed bonnets and outdoor wear, and several outfits for day and evening. If you discovered that your clothes were unfashionable, it was possible to have a dress made up for you in just a couple of days. On visits in her early twenties, Jane took the opportunity to replenish her wardrobe and to purchase clothes on behalf of friends and family back home – shoes, stockings, lace. Indeed, in spite of the occasional sardonic aside, her letters suggest that she enjoyed both the retail therapy and the social whirl.

There was a hospital offering free accommodation to those who had come to Bath to restore their health, and servants and those on low incomes were charged lower fees to bathe, but the city wasn't somewhere you would choose to go if finances

Libraries

One decided advantage of towns, for both Austen and a number of her characters, was their libraries. Most books remained expensive to purchase. When the Austen family moved to Bath, they sold 200 volumes. This would have been considered a reasonably impressive private collection, and would have cost a good deal of money to build up (hence the desire to recoup some of it), but it represented a fraction of the books that were then available. Much of the Austen family library would have consisted of Latin and Greek texts, and presumably there would also have been some books of theological interest. Though the family were happy to read novels, they will mostly have been borrowed ones. It's unlikely that they owned more than a handful.

Commercial libraries were businesses and gave readers what they wanted: choice and variety for a manageable subscription. We might think of them as the equivalent of streaming services and they were similarly revolutionary; rather than saving up to buy a couple of albums or books a year, you could browse among thousands, and try several every month. You could take out a volume of sermons if you wanted, but there was also biography, history, poetry, and novels. Even in a small town, a library might offer 3,000 books, while the largest of the London libraries had 20,000. Publishers pivoted to producing the kind of novels that libraries wanted: stirring stories in multi-volume formats so that one novel could be rented out to several subscribers simultaneously.

Catherine Morland is introduced to 'horrid' novels in Bath. Her new friend recommends a long list of popular commercial titles that would have been readily accessible from Bath's libraries. In her fiction Austen shows libraries as an exciting resource, offering education, entertainment and, crucially, choice – something which was lacking for many women. Bored housewife Mary Musgrove is enlivened by the library in Lyme Regis. Fanny Price, in *Mansfield Park*, finds few pleasures when she is sent to stay with her impoverished birth family in Portsmouth, but one is the local 'circulating library'. 'She became a subscriber,' Austen tells us, 'amazed to be a renter, a chuser [sic] of books!' The Bennet girls are library members, and almost the first thing that the heroine of *Sanditon* does, on arriving at the seaside resort, is to visit the library.

As well as lending books, Georgian libraries often sold hats, jewellery, souvenirs, cosmetics, medicines and lottery tickets; they were places for dreaming and fantasy, where the imagination could range freely. And as fans of Austen, we have reason to be grateful to them. We'll see that for a long period in the 1820s and 1830s, public awareness of her books was preserved largely by libraries and library subscribers.

'The Library of course afforded every thing; all the useless things in the World that could not be done without, and among so many pretty Temptations [...] Charlotte began to feel that she must check herself [...] so, she turned from Drawers of rings and Broches repressed farther solicitation and paid for what she bought'

Sanditon

Left Isaac Cruikshank, detail from *The Circulating Library*, 1804. Libraries helped revolutionize the way people read.

were very tight. It was cheaper than London, however, and somewhere it was easy to budget. With a couple of moderate subscription payments – to the Pump Room, say, and the Upper Assembly Rooms – you could be assured of activities and agreeable society. In *Persuasion*, the debt-ridden Sir Walter is persuaded to move to Bath rather than the capital when renting out his country estate, because 'he might there be important at comparatively little expense'.

Bath was a small city, the kind of place people would have been continually meeting or passing one another, even if so many of them hadn't been operating on the same daily schedule. It quickly became a popular place to socialize but it was also potentially a risky one. Ordinarily, you could gauge someone's wealth and standing by the amount of land they owned, their house and their social circle. But in Bath most visitors were staying in rented accommodation or hotels and frequenting the same places. When you arrived, you introduced yourself to the master of ceremonies and wrote your name in his book. The idea was that he would be able to judge your social position and place you with your own kind of people, but a superficial appearance of affluence and respectability could take you a long way. In *Persuasion*, Sir Walter's cousin William Elliot bears a questionable character with some of his former friends and is in financial difficulty, but in Bath he passes for an 'agreeable',

Above Thomas Rowlandson, *The gig shop, or kicking up a breese at Nell Hamilton's hop*, 1811. Regency ballrooms were not always as genteel as we imagine.

An Easy Cure;
or, a Prescription for an Invalid when at Bath

If, brother Hyp, you want a cure
At Bath, a lodging warm secure;
There drink the wholesome stream by rule,
When nature's stream runs low and cool.

Arise betime, to pump repair;
First take the water, then the air;
Next strole to coffee-house, peruse
With air of negligence the news;

Not caring whether party rules,
Provided no rebellious tools
Disturb the nation's publick peace,
To interrupt your private ease.

Frequent your church in decent dress,
Yourself to none but God address;
There offer up religious vows,
Avoiding foppish forms and bows.

When you've your due devotion paid,
Walk on the North or South-Parade;
If weather's clear, in sun and air,
The best of whets – for food prepare.

Then sparing take of lightest kind,
To keep the vessels free from wind:
In wine and sauces don't exceed;
Luxurious tastes distempers breed.

Nature refresh'd, let nature rest;
With inward peace your mind digest;
Digestion's work is easiest wrought
By cheerful chat and little thought.

Or, to disperse black fumes away,
At Whist or Ombre [card games] cheerful play;
Be unconcern'd at loss or gain, –
A spirit ruffled raises pain.

The mind unbent, your thoughts prepare
To bear a part in ev'ning prayer:
That duty done, a draught repeat;
Concoction help with liquid heat.

Then lounge at Coffee-house in chat
On various themes of God knows what,
'Till two or more of friendly kind,
Of nature good, of cheerful mind,

In sense and mirth agree to pass
The time till nine in circling glad:
Then home to sleep; and rise next light,
With spirits lively, gay, and bright.

Thus invalids, from day to day,
Must keep, like clocks, in constant way;
Must moderate be in meat and drink,
And rarely (very rarely) think;

Must exercise, with gentle force,
On foot, or coach, or pacing horse;
Must rise and set at early hours,
And ne'er exert beyond their pow'rs.

This course observ'd, will thousands save
From pain, from anguish, and the grave. –
Pills nature vex, and weaken too,
These rules of health the man renew.

'I am just returned from my Airing in the very bewitching Phaeton and four', letter from Jane Austen to her sister Cassandra

'estimable man' and even the cautious heroine Anne deems him 'their pleasantest acquaintance' in the city and assumes he is well-off. Nor were the assemblies always as genteel as might be imagined. Jane describes in a letter to Cassandra in May 1801 how one evening at the 'upper rooms' she saw both 'an Adultress' [sic] (a Miss Twistleton, who was in fact a distant cousin of hers) and another woman who was chasing 'round the room after her drunken husband'; 'his avoidance, & her pursuit, with the probable intoxication of both, was,' she writes, 'an amusing scene'.

The constant proximity and continual re-encounters that Bath enabled made it somewhere new acquaintances were easily formed and rapidly developed, as Austen shows in *Northanger Abbey*, where Catherine Morland and Isabella Thorpe become best friends within a very short period of meeting. And the fact that so much of the daily routine was communal, carried out in full public view, sometimes lulled parents and guardians into a false sense of security: in *Sense and Sensibility*, it's in Bath that Colonel Brandon's young ward Eliza is seduced by Willoughby, she and her school friend having been 'ranging all over the town and making what acquaintance they chose'. Catherine Morland makes friends with the Tilney family in Bath and is permitted to pay a visit to their home, which she is later effectively thrown out of. Writing during one visit to the city in 1801, Austen mentions that she drove out in a 'bewitching Phaeton & four' with Mr Evelyn, a man whom she cannot have known all that well. 'I really beleive [sic] he is very harmless' she writes to her sister, adding, with startling insouciance that, 'people do not seem afraid of him'.

Opposite James Gillray, *What can Little T.O. do?*, 1801. A phaeton-and-four – a dashing, fashionable way to travel.

Below The church of St Swithin's Walcot in Bath, where Austen's parents were married, and where her father and maternal grandfather are buried.

Crime

By eight o'clock in the morning, the courtroom at the Taunton Assizes was full to capacity. Hundreds of people had crowded in, eager to hear one case in particular on this Saturday 29 March 1800: that of a well-to-do woman in her fifties who stood accused of having stolen a length of lace from a shop in Bath the previous summer, a crime which technically carried the death penalty.

The accused was Mrs Leigh Perrot, who was married to Jane Austen's uncle, James. According to the *Bath Journal*, she was accompanied to the dock by her husband and by a 'Mrs Whinstone and Mrs Chumley of Bath and some other ladies'. A few weeks before, she had written to a cousin, lamenting that none of the Austens would be able to attend her trial, not even James Austen, who nursed expectations from his rich uncle and aunt, but was stuck in Hampshire with a broken leg. Mrs Austen had previously offered her daughters as companions while their aunt was on remand, however, and it is possible that Jane and Cassandra were in fact among these unnamed 'other ladies'. The 'Mrs Chumley' who came to support Mrs Leigh Perrot is likely to have been a connection of her own (her maiden name, Cholmeley, was spelt in a variety of ways) and it would have been foolhardy of the Austens to have neglected to offer their support.

Mrs Leigh Perrot's social status meant that she received favourable treatment. Assizes – court trials for serious offences – were mobile, moving from town to town, and so only came to an area at widely spaced intervals. Rather than spending the eight long months of waiting in prison, though, Mrs Leigh Perrot was confined in the prison governor's house, and her husband was permitted to remain with her. She was far more fortunate than most of those accused of serious crimes, who could be left in terrible conditions. Prison hygiene, catering and discipline were lamentable, and serious illness and assaults on prisoners all too common.

The Leigh Perrots were able to pay for a number of lawyers, and to convince several elite character witnesses to appear, including the then Lord Braybrooke and two members of parliament. Unless several of the other witnesses had been suborned, though, the likeliest explanation seems to be that the shopkeepers had been attempting blackmail, and perhaps not for the first time. Customers came forward to testify that when unwrapping parcels from the same shop, they had discovered goods they had neither ordered nor paid for. A 'not guilty' verdict was returned by a jury chiefly composed of respectable small businessmen, whose natural sympathies are likelier to have lain with the shopkeeper rather than the customer. After eight months of incarceration, and seven hours in court, Mrs Leigh Perrot was free to return home.

That ought to have been the end of the matter, but it wasn't. Every detail of the trial was reported. An article on the case appeared in the *Ladies' Magazine*, together with what purported to be a portrait of Mrs Leigh Perrot. Two pamphlets were published, one featuring a diagram of the shop floor so that readers could follow the evidence more easily. It took years for the scandal to die away. In 1806, when James Leigh Perrot was mentioned in the will of a relation, the *Oracle and Daily Advertiser* newspaper reminded their readers that he was 'husband of the Lady who was tried on suspicion of concealing and carrying away some lace'.

Not everyone was convinced that she was innocent. Doubts must have been expressed and rumours swirled about. There is a story claiming Mrs Leigh Perrot was caught in the act of shoplifting a second time and suggestions that she was an habitual thief, even a kleptomaniac, but the truth of the matter is lost.

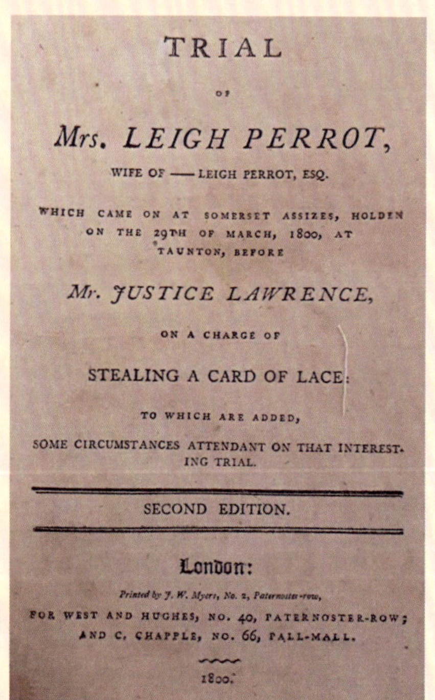

TRIAL

OF

Mrs. LEIGH PERROT,

WIFE OF —— LEIGH PERROT, ESQ.

WHICH CAME ON AT SOMERSET ASSIZES, HOLDEN ON THE 29TH OF MARCH, 1800, AT TAUNTON, BEFORE

Mr. JUSTICE LAWRENCE,

ON A CHARGE OF

STEALING A CARD OF LACE:

TO WHICH ARE ADDED,

SOME CIRCUMSTANCES ATTENDANT ON THAT INTERESTING TRIAL.

SECOND EDITION.

London:

Printed by J. W. Myers, No. 2, Paternoster-row,

FOR WEST AND HUGHES, NO. 40, PATERNOSTER-ROW; AND C. CHAPPLE, NO. 66, PALL-MALL.

1800.

Right A pamphlet entitled *The trial of Mrs. Leigh Perrot*. Published in 1800.

Right 'Mrs Leigh Perrot', 1800, a picture purporting to be of Jane's aunt which accompanied the report of the trial in the *Lady's Magazine*.

Jane may have felt that Bath was familiar, safe. The family had long-standing connections there. Her parents probably met in Oxford, but it was in Bath that they got married, in 1764, at St Swithin's Church, Walcot. Her grandfather was buried in the same church. Mrs Austen's brother James Leigh Perrot and his wife had also married in Bath. He had added 'Perrot' to his name in order to inherit from a relation and his wife was an heiress, so they could easily afford to live between their Berkshire property, Scarlets, and a house in Bath at No. 1 The Paragon. When Jane visited, she usually stayed with her uncle and aunt or, on one occasion, with her rich brother Edward, who rented No. 13 Queen Square.

In 1801, however, Mr and Mrs Austen decided to leave their home in Steventon and move to Bath. There were points in favour of the move but the timing is surprising: it was, after all, just the year before that Mrs Leigh Perrot had been tried for stealing lace from a shop in Bath and the public scandal hadn't yet died down. Possibly the Austens wanted to offer visible moral support to the Leigh Perrots, who were close relations, and, more to point, rich and childless ones. They may also have hoped to find husbands for Cassandra and Jane, since neither was yet thirty.

Two broken engagements

In December 1802, just before Jane's twenty-seventh birthday, she supposedly got engaged to a young man named Harris Bigg Wither. She'd known him for years as the little brother of her friends Alethea, Catherine and Elizabeth Bigg; they had been near-neighbours. Jane and Cassandra, by then living in Bath, had been invited to Manydown Park for a visit. Perhaps Jane was simply overjoyed to be back home in Hampshire, or perhaps she was influenced by Harris's excellent prospects and thoughts of the large, comfortable house he would one day inherit. Wine might have been drunk, older sisters may have been meddling. At any rate – so the story goes – Harris proposed and Jane accepted. The following morning she went down and informed everyone that she had made a mistake. She and Cassandra left Manydown and returned to Bath. Their mother, when she learned what had happened, was, Mrs Bennet-like, both furious and utterly unable to comprehend Jane's decision, but there doesn't seem, from what we can gather, to have been any lasting awkwardness between the two families.

The information comes to us at several removes. Jane's nephew, James Edward Austen-Leigh, included it (without giving names) in his *A Memoir of Jane Austen*, published in the late 1860s. He had heard it from his sister Caroline, and *she* had pieced it together from diary entries their mother had written, and comments made years afterwards. While this is hardly evidence that would stand up in court, that doesn't mean the story is baseless. It's proved attractive to many, partly because, in contrast to Austen's brief and often slightly unsatisfying depictions of successful proposals, she writes a cracking rejection scene, and partly because we want to believe that someone who had so much to say about the struggle between romance and prudence, love and caution, understood what she was writing about.

Austen does show some sympathy to a character like Charlotte Lucas, who marries purely for financial reasons and finds herself paying a price for it. We have no real idea, though, whether this has any connection to Harris, or exactly what, if anything, happened.

Though he doesn't appear to have pined, Harris also didn't move on to the next candidate with the unseemly haste of a Mr Collins. He married towards the end of 1804, some two years after the date usually given for the short-lived engagement between him and Jane. Jane, meanwhile, turned her mind back to her writing, and set herself seriously to the business of finding a publisher.

And she found one. In 1803 Crosby and Co. accepted her novel *Susan (Northanger Abbey)* for publication, paying £10 for the copyright. This wasn't much, but the risks were all the publisher's, and Austen was an unknown. The approach appears to have been made via a legal acquaintance of Henry Austen; perhaps he didn't bother to drive a harder bargain. While not generous, Crosby was a perfectly reputable outfit, which produced both useful and entertaining books, including plenty aimed at younger readers. *Susan* wasn't a bad fit for them. The book was advertised in the newspapers as being 'in the press', that is, in the process of being printed, several times during the summer of 1803 but it didn't appear.

Right Manydown Park in the 1960s. Jane knew the house as the home of the Bigg family. Tradition claims that she accepted a proposal from the only son, Harris, but changed her mind.

'She disliked Bath,
and did not think it agreed with her.'

Persuasion

We're often told Jane disliked Bath. Actually, though that's true of one of her heroines, Anne Elliot, Jane seems to have enjoyed at least some aspects of her earlier visits. Few letters survive from the four years when she was based there – not enough to arrive at any kind of firm conclusion about her feelings. We know that there was a lot going on in her life, though. Between a possible brief engagement in 1802, her friend Anne Lefroy's fatal riding accident in December 1804, and the death of her father just a few weeks later in January 1805, this was an emotionally gruelling time for her. There was the pleasure and excitement of having a novel accepted for publication in 1803, and then the dawning disappointment when it failed to appear. As Austen has her heroine say in *Persuasion*, however, '"One does not love a place the less for having suffered in it, unless it has been all suffering, nothing but suffering [...]"'.

The Austens collected a large social circle in Bath and at least some of their extended family looked them up when they came to the city, so it doesn't seem that they were lonely or isolated, or that their association with the locally notorious Mrs Leigh Perrot – or the adulterous Miss Twistleton – did them any harm.

Bath wasn't somewhere the Austens lived all year round. They went on holidays and paid lengthy visits to friends and family, returning to occupy several different Bath rental properties. They spent three years at 4 Sydney Place, then took shorter leases on 27 Green Park Buildings, 25 Gay Street and lodgings in Trim Street. The addresses have their own tale to tell: that money was never very plentiful, and that finances got tighter, particularly once Mr Austen died. The rent of Sydney Place was, according to advertisements placed at the time, 'very low': it was a sublet. When they were first looking for accommodation, the Austens had dismissed Green Park Buildings as damp and unhealthy, but they still ended up living there – and in the case of Mr Austen, dying there. Trim Street would not have been considered particularly desirable for the family, being close to the theatre, and home to several business premises and a non-conformist chapel.

It may have been during these years in Bath that Jane wrote the fragment known as *The Watsons*, a story centring on the unmarried daughters of a clergyman who are already growing anxious about what will happen to them after his death. Jane's encounters with the horse-mad Mr Evelyn do seem to have helped to inspire John Thorpe in *Northanger Abbey*. Anne Elliot, in *Persuasion*, associates the town with the loss of her mother, and that novel also takes us into less salubrious parts of Bath, such as Westgate Buildings, just around the corner from Trim Street, where Anne's old school friend lives, 'in a very humble way', confined to 'a noisy parlour, and a dark bedroom behind'.

It is generally doubted that Jane wrote much during her late twenties, and the circumstances don't look as if they would have been particularly conducive to it; but wherever she found herself, in the Pump Room or cramped lodgings, at the seaside or a parsonage house, in a town or on a country estate, she was collecting material.

Countryside

"'When I am in the country," he replied, "I never wish to leave it [...]'"

Pride and Prejudice

Though Austen isn't an exclusively rural writer, some of her most famous fictional settings are in the countryside, often on large estates. Mr Darcy's 'beautiful estate at Pemberley' in *Pride and Prejudice* is the best known, but there are also Northanger Abbey and Mansfield Park and Kellynch, Donwell and Sotherton, besides the smaller or less prominent estates like Longbourn, Netherfield, Fullerton, Enscombe, Randalls, Uppercross and Winthrop. Austen's first published novel, *Sense and Sensibility*, includes a very large number, several of them in close proximity. There's Norland and Barton, and also Stanhill, Delaford, Allenham, Whitwell, Combe Magna and Cleveland.

Estates were businesses – both agricultural holding and rental portfolio – but they were also part of the nation and of the established order in a way other businesses were not. Wealth gained from industry, trade and banking was still considered less than ideal in Austen's world. So too were fortunes derived from Britain's colonial holdings overseas or from enslaved labour in the Caribbean. This was less because of ethical concerns (though, as we will see, these weren't entirely absent) and more because new money was disruptive – granting power and influence but detached from the structures through which that usually flowed. Use your fortune to buy land, though, and you could begin to be woven into a web of mutual obligation and local relationships.

Votes were not private at this point and so the owner of a country estate, being able to influence their tenants, might in effect have several, and groups of neighbours could work together to sway the outcome of an election. There were even landowners whose estates included entire parliamentary boroughs and who were in the position to more or less choose whichever member of parliament they preferred.

Opposite Lyme, in Cheshire, which featured as Pemberley in the 1995 adaptation of *Pride and Prejudice*.

Below James Gillray, *Middlesex-election, 1804*, 1804. Elections were chaotic, even though few people had the vote.

Opposite 'Harrow, while poaching, discovered by the Gamekeeper'. An illustration for the popular book *The Newgate Calendar*. Harrow was a highwayman as well, but he could have been executed as a poacher. Hunting wild animals often constituted a crime – but only if you were too poor to buy a licence.

All kinds of rights were only available to those who owned or rented houses or land worth more than a certain amount. Becoming a local justice of the peace or sitting on a jury were also property-dependent. If your family held a reasonably sized property, then you could get a certificate permitting you to shoot pheasants and partridges; if they didn't, then the same actions were criminalized, potentially punishable by transportation to Australia or death. It was also perfectly legal to target poachers and trespassers with man traps capable of breaking or mangling a leg. In a very early piece of writing called *Jack and Alice*, Jane jokes about this happening to one of her characters.

The television and heritage industries have made it easy to think of country estates as being leisured places, tranquil and orderly, but during Austen's lifetime very little was tranquil. And at this point, keeping an estate going required an enormous amount of labour – field labourers, shepherds and cowmen, dairymaids and gamekeepers, gardeners, grooms for the stables and all the indoor servants, as well as a management tier of housekeepers, stewards and bailiffs. An estate owner might be not just employer and landlord, but also judge and jury and member of parliament, or friends with those who were. Often they also had the right to select the local vicar, as we see several times in Austen's novels. In a small community, the gap between people with power and privilege and people without was obvious, unbridgeable and, with revolutionary sentiment spreading, dangerous.

As war consumed Europe, British tourists were largely restricted to seeing the sights of their own country: the hills, the lakes, the grand houses, and the 'manufactories', but also, in passing, as they travelled along, rural poverty, inequality and squalor. The political debates that swirled around almost every subject didn't leave the countryside untouched – far from it.

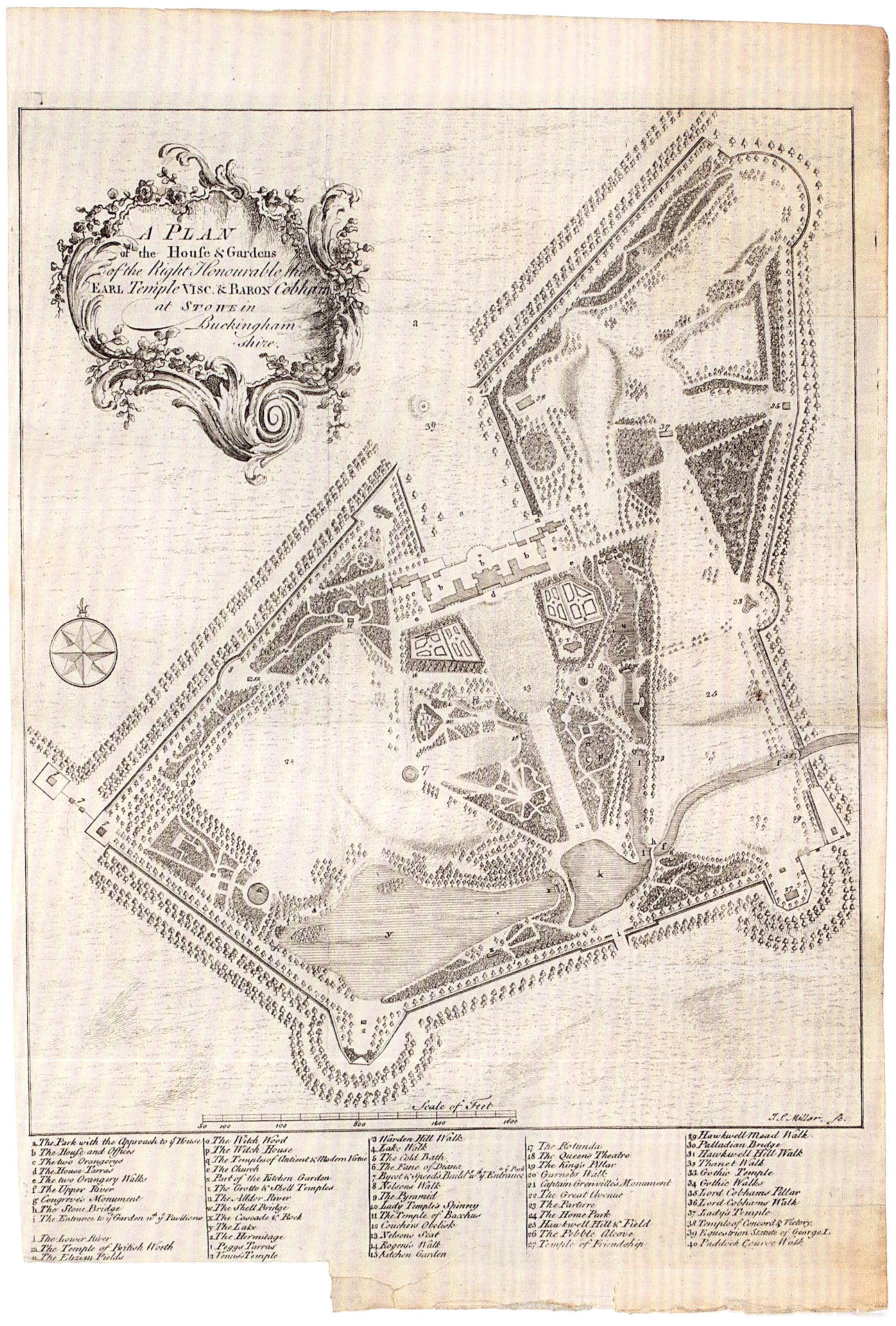
A PLAN
of the House & Gardens
of the Right Honourable the
EARL Temple VISC. & BARON Cobham
at STOWE in
Buckingham
shire.
Scale of Feet
J. C. Miller. sc.
a The Park with the Approach to ye House
b The House and Offices
c The two Orangerys
d The House Tarras
e The two Orangery Walks
f The Upper River
g Congreve's Monument
h The Stone Bridge
i The Entrance to ye Garden wth ye Pavilions
l The Lower River
m The Temple of British Worth
n The Elizian Fields
o The Witch Wood
p The Witch House
q The Temples of Antient & Modern Virtue
r The Church
s Part of the Kitchen Garden
t The Grotto & Shell Temples
u The Allder River
w The Shell Bridge
x The Cascade & Rock
y The Lake
z The Hermitage
1 Peggs Tarras
2 Venus Temple
3 Warden Hill Walk
4 Lake Walk
5 The Cold Bath
6 The Fane of Diana
7 Bycot & Speeds Build wth ye Entrance to ye Park
8 Nelsons Walk
9 The Pyramid
10 Lady Temple's Spinny
11 The Temple of Baxchus
12 Couchers Obelisk
13 Nelsons Seat
14 Rogers's Walk
15 Kitchen Garden
17 The Rotunda
18 The Queen's Theatre
19 The King's Pillar
20 Gurnets Walk
21 Captain Grenville's Monument
22 The Great Avenue
23 The Parterre
24 The Home Park
25 Hawkwell Hill & Field
26 The Pebble Alcove
27 Temple of Friendship
29 Hawkwell Mead Walk
30 Palladian Bridge
31 Hawkwell Hill Walk
32 Thanet Walk
33 Gothic Temple
34 Gothic Walks
35 Lord Cobhams Pillar
36 Lord Cobhams Walk
37 Lady's Temple
38 Temple of Concord & Victory
39 Equestrian Statute of George I.
40 Paddock Course Walk

Opposite 'A plan of the house and gardens at Stowe', from a guidebook produced by Benton Seeley, 1766.

Austen quite often uses estates as a way of explaining character, as well as bringing in politics. Pemberley is a handsome house situated in a large park, but it's more significant that the furniture is tasteful, not showy, and that Mr Darcy's housekeeper praises him as '"the best landlord and the best master"', claiming that '"There is not one of his tenants or servants but what will give him a good name"' and expressing her belief that he will be '"just as affable to the poor"' as his father was before him. We seem to be meant to contrast this with Rosings, with its many expensive windows and air of excessive 'splendour', and with Darcy's aunt Lady Catherine who, 'when any of the cottagers were disposed to be quarrelsome, discontented or too poor [...] sallied forth into the village to [...] silence their complaints, and scold them into harmony and plenty'.

Significant too is the description of the grounds at Pemberley. There is a 'lodge' at the entrance – a small house sometimes occupied by a gatekeeper. Then comes a 'beautiful wood, stretching over a wide extent' of rising ground, and a valley, through which the road winds 'with some abruptness'.

From the middle of the eighteenth century onwards there was a trend for landscaping estate grounds, creating large expanses of labour-intensive lawn and views to grazing livestock kept at a distance by invisible boundaries like ha-has (sunken ditches or fences which animals were unable to cross). Artificial or artificially assisted lakes and water features were popular, as were ornate stone bridges. Often extensive earthworks were undertaken to shut out or open up a view. 'Belts' of woodland were planted around the boundaries, and clumps of trees and garden 'follies' (Grecian-style temples, for example, or fake ruins) carefully positioned to draw the eye. Sometimes buildings or even roads were moved, while driveways traced gentle curves through the parkland to show off the house at its best angles.

Pemberley, though, doesn't have ornamental 'belts' and clumps of trees: it has established woods, stretching over 'a wide extent' and including at least one area of 'rough coppice-wood', regularly cut back so that it can be used. The driveway winds, but it does so abruptly. Elizabeth's walk around the grounds takes her across a bridge that is 'simple', not ornate. There appear to be no follies and though in places the 'opening of the trees' offers 'charming views of the valley', the effect seems accidental rather than painstakingly planned.

This is not to say there has been no landscaping. There is a lawn, so the grounds aren't old-fashioned. In front of the house we're told that 'a stream of some natural importance was swelled into greater' – dammed to form a wider, more aesthetically appealing, shape. This has been done 'without any artificial appearance', however, and the river is still teeming with fish, offering both 'sport' and food. The implication is that the Darcy family had the money to landscape, but the good taste and good sense not to overdo it. The grounds have been gently and economically updated rather than fully (and expensively) remodelled. An admiring Elizabeth thinks that she 'had never seen a place for which nature had done more, or where natural beauty had been so little counteracted by an awkward taste'. The estate is beautiful, but it remains natural and productive. Lizzy jokes that she dates her falling in love with Darcy '"from [...] first seeing his beautiful grounds at Pemberley"', but the house and its surroundings really do enable her to learn a lot about him.

Jane Austen's forebears had owned quite a lot of land. Like nearly all the money, the land went to other relations, but she did end up living on one family estate – Chawton, in Hampshire – and visiting others: Godmersham Park in Kent which came into the ownership of her brother Edward, and also Stoneleigh Abbey in Warwickshire and Adlestrop House in Gloucestershire, which were inherited by cousins of her mother. Godmersham, which Austen knew from the late 1790s, has been suggested at various times as the model for Rosings, Pemberley, Mansfield Park and Sotherton.

Rosings is also located in Kent and visible from the road, as Godmersham was, but Austen places it near the town of Westerham, which is about fifty miles away. Like Pemberley, Godmersham is nestled in a valley with a river (the Stour), but according to the description of the estate in Edward Hasted's *The History and Topographical Survey of the County of Kent*, the two would have looked quite different. Godmersham had been thoroughly and fashionably landscaped, with a 'temple', a 'sunk fence' (a ha-ha) along the east side of the park, 'sheep walks' visible in the distance and trees 'at proper intervals'. It also apparently had both a wilderness (an area of densely planted woodland with meandering paths) and an avenue of trees. There's an extended episode in *Mansfield Park* set at the estate of Sotherton, where both a wilderness and an avenue feature prominently, as do a ha-ha and a fence.

Austen seems in fact to have drawn inspiration for *Mansfield Park* not just from Godmersham, but also from Adlestrop and Stoneleigh. Adlestrop House had been owned by Jane's mother's family since the middle of the sixteenth century. The nearby parsonage was owned by them too, and many generations of family members had served as vicars. During Austen's lifetime the vicar there was the second son, the living set aside for him as the estate had been for his older brother, just as happens in *Mansfield Park*. A stronger

link comes, though, from the fact that both the Adlestrop estate and the grounds of the parsonage had been landscaped – 'improved' – by the most famous landscape gardener of the late eighteenth and early nineteenth century: Humphrey Repton. Jane, who visited Adlestrop in 1794, 1799 and 1806, would have been able to observe some of the changes he made.

Mansfield Park is fascinated by the topic of improvements. Everyone is doing it or talking about it: making a 'plantation to shut out the churchyard', envying a friend who has 'recently had his grounds laid out by an improver', planning the 'removal' of a 'farmyard', complaining about the 'dirt and confusion' of 'improvements' in progress. Three chapters are devoted to a visit to the large but old-fashioned estate of Sotherton to discuss possible changes to it. Repton is mentioned by name several times.

In 1806, when Mrs Austen's cousin Thomas Leigh inherited the large and old-fashioned Stoneleigh Abbey, Jane and her mother travelled there with him. Stoneleigh had a chapel, like Sotherton does, and it, too, has links to Repton, whom Thomas Leigh employed to remodel the grounds there as he had done at Adlestrop.

Repton was famous for his 'Red Books' – part surveyor's report, part sales brochure, bound in red leather – which featured beautiful fold-out illustrations; the 'before' scene appeared on a flap which could be turned back to reveal how it would look after his improvements. The red book Repton made for Adlestrop doesn't survive, but the one for Stoneleigh does.

Above Humphrey Repton, a plan for one of his highly-stylized landscapes from the *Red Book* for Ferney Hall, *c.*1789.

Chawton

In 1809, eight years after she had moved away from the Hampshire countryside, Jane moved back there, to a cottage in the village of Chawton. She would remain living there for the rest of her life, together with her mother and Cassandra and their long-term friend Martha Lloyd (whose sister Mary was married to James Austen and who would herself later marry the widowed Frank Austen). Chawton was one of the estates that had come to Edward Austen from his adoptive parents. He owned a number of houses and we don't know why he hadn't offered to accommodate his sisters and their widowed mother before this point. The cottage had recently come free, having previously been occupied by the estate bailiff, and was of a particularly manageable size. Edward did it up for them. Another attraction was that it brought them closer – albeit not very close – to family. James and his family still occupied the rectory house in Steventon, while Thomas Leigh and George Austen continued to make their home in Monk Sherborne.

The rate at which Austen wrote and published during the eight years she was at Chawton is generally believed to show how happy she was there. The house itself pleased her – she wrote a poem just after she moved which announces that the cottage 'will all other houses beat'. She also took to the surroundings.

These days Chawton is marooned on one side of the A31 and feels like a bit of a backwater; like Steventon, it was better connected when Jane lived there than it is today. A turnpike road ran through the middle of the village and coaches passed daily, right outside the windows of the cottage. Jane often walked the short distance to the town of Alton – again, something which was easier then. There was nevertheless beautiful countryside round about. Chawton is now on the edge of the South Downs National Park and the writer and naturalist Gilbert White, who lived in nearby Selborne in the eighteenth century, lovingly describes the local 'hill, dale, wood-lands' and 'heath', not to mention the wildlife. Selborne Common remained unenclosed.

In an 1814 letter to her niece Anna, who was trying her hand at a novel, Jane suggested that '3 or 4 families in a Country Village is the very thing to work on'. That description doesn't, however, fit all of her own novels very well. It seems that she found her time in other places more intellectually and artistically stimulating, but Chawton was somewhere she seems to have felt at home and it was where she was able to write.

[...] As for ourselves, we're very well,
As unaffected prose will tell.
Cassandra's pen will give our state
The many comforts that await
Our Chawton Home – how much we find
Already in it to our mind,
And how convinced that when complete,
It will all other houses beat,
That ever have been made or mended,
With rooms concise or rooms distended. [...]

Above The cottage in Chawton that was home to Jane Austen from 1809 until 1817, now a museum.

'She had never seen a place for which nature had done more, or where natural beauty had been so little counteracted by an awkward taste.'

Pride and Prejudice

Below Detail from a picture showing St Nicholas' Church and Chawton House, owned by Jane's brother Edward, c.1850.

Right William Gilpin, *Two Men Walking in a Lansdscape*, 1783. The picturesque tended to prioritize aesthetics over individuals.

Below T. Harber, *Adlestrop Park, Gloucestershire*, c.1830, after John Preston Neale. Jane knew Adlestrop well and the improvements there may have helped to inspire parts of *Mansfield Park*.

'She sat in silence almost all the way [...] except when any object of picturesque beauty within their view drew from her an exclamation of delight [...]'

Sense and Sensibility

Repton aimed at a naturalistic effect, but his plans often required extensive labour and artifice. He would draw up diagrams with sightlines and angles of reflection, and give instructions on exactly how to plant and prune trees so that they would grow into the desired shapes. He thought in terms of creating scenes that could come from paintings and was influenced by 'picturesque' ideas.

The picturesque was both an art style and a way of responding to and talking about landscapes, popularized by the artist and author William Gilpin, who published nearly a dozen books on the subject. Several of these took readers through 'picturesque' areas of Britain – north Wales, the Lake District, the Highlands, the New Forest – and found increased favour as Europe became too risky for tourists. Gilpin admired tumbledown cottages, interestingly gnarled trees, ruins and rocky cliffs, and disliked cultivated farmland and cities, unless viewed from a distance. There's a degree of overlap with the romantic poetry of William Wordsworth, much of which features the poet-narrator wandering through wild, lonely country or imagining the unhappy stories of figures glimpsed in the landscape.

According to her brother Henry, Jane was an admirer of Gilpin from her youth, but she wasn't above making fun of some of his more rigid ideas. Elizabeth Bennet anticipates with pleasure the '"rocks and mountains"' she will see on a planned tour to the Lakes, but elsewhere she jokes about Gilpin's insistence that objects should be grouped in threes, telling Darcy and the two Bingley sisters that they are '"charmingly group'd and appear to uncommon advantage"' and that '"The picturesque would be spoiled by admitting a fourth"'.

It's obvious from her fiction that Austen had reservations. Henry Tilney has the picturesque jargon down pat ('fore-grounds, distances and second distances – side-screens and perspectives'). Marianne Dashwood imagines that she is among the few able to appreciate landscape as Gilpin himself did. Both are made to appear, at best, rather pretentious. At one point in *Sense and Sensibility* the usually diffident Edward Ferrars even picks an argument with Marianne on the subject, professing his dislike of '"ruined, tattered cottages"' and '"nettles or thistles or heath blossoms"'. He admires '"a snug farm-house [...] and a troop of tidy, happy villagers"' – a prosperous, productive country scene. This, in a nutshell, was the debate about land during Austen's lifetime: what should be preferred and prioritized?

At times both Gilpin and Repton show a shocking disregard for the people who lived and worked in the countryside. A dilapidated cottage might look interesting, but it wasn't going to be weatherproof. A solitary twisted tree didn't offer much in the way of firewood. In his *Observations on the Theory and Practice of Landscape Gardening* Repton recommends moving most of the 'humble dwellings' of labouring families out of sight, leaving one or two 'that the occasional smoke from the chimnies [sic] may animate the scene'. In the 'Red Books', the figures of working men and women are carefully positioned for artistic effect, reduced almost to garden ornaments.

It may not be a coincidence that *Mansfield Park*, a novel about 'improvements', a novel which mentions Repton, is also the novel in which Austen begins to show greater awareness not just of servants, but also of farmers and estate and agricultural workers – something she continues in *Emma*.

Right Detail from *Tithe Pig*, probably by Thomas Rowlandson, 1790. A rector looks critically at a pig, part of his tithe entitlement. His gouty foot suggests that he is a glutton.

Below William Ward, *The Newbus Ox*, 1812, after Thomas Weaver. Selective breeding advanced quickly in the late 18th and early 19th centuries, helping drive an agricultural revolution.

Austen often refers to the annual income of an estate rather than to its size (Pemberley brings in 'a clear ten thousand per annum') and this is because there wasn't a straightforward, direct relation between the two. Land varied, as did landowners. As well as farming on their own account, estate owners usually drew rent from tenant farmers, and from houses and shops built on their property, but the number and quality of those were to an extent a matter of choice. Some landowners branched out into investing in various local industries or, indeed, further afield, while others elected to plough money back into their estates. In the last decades of the eighteenth century there was a growing interest in bringing more land into agricultural use, and into pursuing new machinery and farming methods. Selective breeding programmes had resulted in hardier animal breeds that could stand greater exposure to the elements. Mr Knightley, in *Emma*, is clearly identified as a modern landowner, seldom happier than when discussing 'the plan of a drain' or 'the change of a fence', '"shows of cattle"' and '"new drills"' (that is, seed drills, machines still in use on arable farms).

In theory all the land in England belongs to the monarch. And in practice every acre, every square inch, does have an owner, sometimes several owners – even open heathland or the wide, wild expanses of Exmoor and Dartmoor. Some pieces of land come with rights over other sections. And in Jane Austen's day the situation was even more complicated than it is now.

Many parish priests were still supported not just by 'glebe', which was land set aside for them to farm, but by something called 'tithes'. Mr Collins is, in *Pride and Prejudice*. Under the tithe system a proportion of parish produce was supposed to be handed over to the local vicar, though tithes could also be owed elsewhere, sometimes even to secular landowners whose property happened to have been held by the church previously. Harvested 100 sheaves of corn from a field? Ten of those were tithe. Made 100 bricks? Reared a litter of piglets? Picked a basket of apples? You were supposed to hand over a proportion of those, too. Unsurprisingly, tithes were unpopular, not just with the people who paid them, but with many on the receiving end; it wasn't always obvious what a clergyman was supposed to do with a miscellaneous collection of goods, some perishable, and collecting them could lead to friction. It was possible to phase out tithes and give the vicar a larger allowance of glebe land instead. At the end of the eighteenth century the process was accelerated, incidental to other, more seismic changes.

In many neighbourhoods there were areas of land where some local inhabitants might have a legal right to plant or to pasture their animals, and often those locals who *weren't* legally entitled made use of the land too. These pieces of land were common fields or commons. The names are a touch misleading because they weren't in fact in common ownership, but they were subject to use by others, and it wasn't usually practical for the actual landowner to attempt to do anything much with them. There was also what was called 'waste', land which for a variety of reasons wasn't considered worth cultivating (the soil might be of poor quality; the ground might be stony or waterlogged or overgrown with bracken). Many landowners were tolerant of the waste being used to collect a small amount of firewood or to pick berries and nuts and mushrooms. Some might even turn a blind eye to an occasional rabbit trap.

Below John Raphael Smith, *Cottage Family*, 1803, after George Morland. The family have been collecting firewood, possibly from nearby common land.

Agricultural labourers were poorly paid and their diet, heavy on carbohydrates and light on protein, was barely nutritionally adequate for the very physical work they did. Women and children worked too, but their labour tended to be seasonal and even less well-remunerated. Keeping a cow, a goat or a goose, or going out to collect firewood or glean food could make a significant difference to people's diet and overall health, as well as saving them money. Common land and waste land was a precious resource. It was also where itinerant groups such as the Roma tended to set up their temporary camps.

But a number of forces began to combine against this state of affairs. One was innovations in farming and in land reclamation, awakening estate owners to the potential that might be hiding in their boggy or shrubby 'waste'. Another was the wars with France, which not only took men out of the rural workforce, but also made importing food into Britain complicated and risky. There were a series of poor harvests in the 1790s, which exacerbated already existing food shortages, and, finally, what was deemed to be an alarming and exponential population growth.

Ranged against Gilpin's picturesque and Repton's artful landscaping came a mounting enthusiasm for making the countryside useful, organized and controlled; for replacing the heathland with wheat fields and filling the mountainsides with sheep. Do away with the old-fashioned, messy system of common and waste land, and use those acres more efficiently, went the argument, and the looming food crisis would be averted. Those with an official right to use the common could be paid off, either in money or with a small personal land allotment, and no one else had a leg to stand on, legally. The hated tithes could be phased out at the same time and other useful changes – like altering the route of a road, or swapping parcels of land about to make better-shaped fields – completed too.

The Roma

Originally from India, the Roma or Romani people have been in Britain since the middle ages. For several centuries they were mistakenly believed to have come from Egypt, giving rise to the older name of 'Gypsies' (now sometimes considered offensive). Traditionally, they travelled around in groups, camping for short periods in different locations; often they timed moves to coincide with horse or cattle fairs or with the various harvests, for which they would offer their labour. They tended to be viewed with suspicion, however, and to frequently find themselves at odds with local inhabitants or with the authorities.

Discriminatory laws were framed against the Roma, and negative attitudes persisted long after these were removed. By many metrics they still remain among the most disadvantaged minority groups in the United Kingdom, perhaps not unrelated to the fact that you can find exoticized or openly racist depictions of Romani characters in British literature well into the twentieth century. In Jane's lifetime even otherwise sensitive and liberal writers expressed deeply unpalatable opinions about them.

The brief scene featuring the Roma in *Emma* is not Jane's finest hour as an author – she shows a woman and a group of children harassing passing pedestrians for money – but in the context of the time, and in comparison with her contemporaries, it is quite mild. And she does suggest that, just like the Highbury locals, these visitors are also affected by enclosure and the changes in the landscape are, for them, wholly negative ones.

Below George Morland, *Landscape with a Gypsy Encampment*, 1790s.

John Clare

During the eighteenth and nineteenth centuries there were several poets from the working class who were published and admired. Sometimes they became celebrities, though few succeeded in building financial security from their writing or found enduring popularity. One such poet who came to fame in the early nineteenth century was John Clare. He was from a family of rural workers and had grown up in a Northamptonshire village, Helpston, which began to be enclosed in 1809.

Enclosure became one of his major poetical themes. He had a deep familiarity with the world he had grown up in – the open fields he wandered across as a boy, the individual trees, the brambles, the summer wildflowers – and watched as it was changed out of all recognition. Enclosure grieved him deeply. It made his own home strange to him. Later in his life, his mental health became very poor and he spent many years living in secure care, but he continued to hanker after the now unreachable places where he had spent his childhood. His poetry offers an insight into the lasting psychological effects that enclosures had, as well as the economic ones.

[...] By Langley Bush I roam but
the bush hath left its hill;

On Cowper Green I stray –
'tis a desert strange and chill –

And spreading Lea Close Oak
ere decay had penned its will

To the axe of the spoiler and self
interest fell a prey;

And Crossberry Way and old Round
Oak's narrow lane

With its hollow trees like pulpits I shall
never see again.

Enclosure like a Bonaparte let not
a thing remain,

It levelled every bush and tree and
levelled every hill

And hung the moles for traitors –
though the brook is running still,

It runs a naked brook, cold and chill. [...]

'Remembrances', John Clare

Below William Hilton, *John Clare*, c.1820-1821. This portrait shows him at the height of his fame as poet.

"'The enclosure of Norland Common, now carrying on, is a most serious drain.'"

Sense and Sensibility

This process was called enclosure and it had been happening sporadically for more than a century, but now the government threw its weight behind changing – modernizing – as many parishes as it could, as fast as possible. Enclosure act after enclosure act passed through parliament; roads were re-routed and landscapes reshaped, trees grubbed up, ditches dug and fences moved. The vicar wouldn't come looking for his tithes anymore, but that chiefly benefited the better off. For poorer parishioners there was to be no more sneaking your animals onto the common, no collecting firewood or gleaning or trapping; after an enclosure had been completed, all that was finished.

The driving idea behind all these enclosures was to grow enough food for everybody. The immediate result, though, was often that people had less to eat as well as less money than before, because they had to buy extra food and fuel. And as shown in the poetry of John Clare, enclosure could also be a deeply traumatic, alienating experience.

Austen had seen an enclosure around Basingstoke, a few miles from Steventon, when she was in her teens. Enclosures are mentioned in passing in several of her novels, and there are what appear to be loaded references to hedges and to farm labourers in *Mansfield Park* and *Persuasion*. But in *Emma* she turns her attention fully on the subject.

Another of Mrs Austen's cousins was married to Samuel Cooke, the vicar of the Surrey village of Great Bookham, near Leatherhead. Mr Cooke was Jane's godfather and Mrs Cooke was a published author. Jane stayed with them on several occasions – they were on the way between London and Hampshire. *The Watsons*, a novel she started and abandoned, is set in Surrey, and one visit seems to have inspired her more directly.

Jane stayed with her cousins in Great Bookham in 1814, where she would have observed the after-effects of the enclosure which had taken place the previous year in the next parish, Fetcham. Highbury, the town in which *Emma* is set, is probably fictional, but its proximity to the beauty spot of Box Hill, and its distance from London, place it firmly in the vicinity and it's clear that, like Fetcham, it too has been recently enclosed. The short-term effects are not positive. A number of the villagers are impoverished, with at least one family dependent on food handouts. Thieves target the 'poultry houses' of local landowners. The visiting Roma, unable to access what used to be common land, are camped at the side of the road, leading to confrontation with passers-by.

Jane never had anything larger than a garden under her control, but she was born and brought up in the countryside. Her father farmed; her brother and uncle and cousins owned estates of varying sizes. Like Gilpin and Repton, and many of her own characters, she appreciated the beauties of the rural landscape, but she also understood that it wasn't perfect, and couldn't remain unchanged.

Seaside

*'They went to the sands,
to watch the flowing of the tide [...]'*

Persuasion

It is paradoxical that the British seaside should have become popular when it did, at the end of the eighteenth century and beginning of the nineteenth. At its narrowest point, the English Channel is just a touch over twenty miles wide. On a clear day, France is visible with the naked eye. And France, for much of Austen's lifetime, was the enemy, mounting several invasion attempts against the British Isles. That it became the fashion during that same period to walk on the shore, go pleasure sailing and bathe in the sea is perhaps best understood as a form of denial, or defiance. Among the most expensive of the British seaside resorts was Brighton, favoured by the Prince Regent, which offered all manner of amusements – the theatre, a promenade, assembly rooms for dances, libraries, a gentlemen's club. But the men's sea-bathing area was located below a gun battery and, even in the absence of the summer army training camps, there was a permanent barracks just outside the town. On one hill was a signal tower, and on another, as back-up, a beacon kept to spread the alarm, should it be needed.

Altogether, Austen spent a fair amount of time on the coast. She was there briefly as a little girl, when her teacher took her and her sister and their cousin to Southampton, and she returned to live in the same town for about two and a half years as an adult, from the autumn of 1806 to the spring of 1809. During the years in Bath, Austen had also visited coastal resorts – among them Lyme Regis in 1804 and Worthing in 1805 – but with two brothers in the Royal Navy, she was unable to view the sea simply as a pretty, health-giving backdrop. Her novels express a kind of double vision: the seaside is associated with leisure and pleasure but there are often dangers lurking, and reminders of the war. Brighton is full of soldiers, Lyme Regis of naval officers. One character nearly falls off a boat at Weymouth, another

Opposite James Gillray, detail from *A Squall*, 1810.

Opposite Thomas Rowlandson, *Portsmouth Point*, c.1814.

encounters a scoundrel at the Kent coastal resort of Ramsgate. The seaside is where Lydia Bennet is seduced in *Pride and Prejudice*, and where, in *Persuasion*, a young woman suffers a traumatic brain injury.

Save for a brief joke about the 'stinking fish of Southampton' in one of her teenage stories, *Love and Freindship* [sic], Austen doesn't mention the town in her fiction, but presumably it was her experience of living there that informed her descriptions of Portsmouth in *Mansfield Park*. Portsmouth was twenty miles away, near where Southampton Water joins the Solent, the channel between the south coast and the Isle of Wight. There was a good deal of movement back and forth between the two, however, and both were dock towns; they were fortified and garrisoned, and served as staging posts for sending troops overseas. Austen doesn't neglect to sketch these details in. *Mansfield Park* describes how the heroine, returning to Portsmouth, the town of her birth, enters it by crossing over a 'draw-bridge'. When she goes for walks, she is forced to resort to the dockyard and the 'ramparts'.

The choice of the Portsmouth setting is unusual. Austen tends not to set scenes in real-life locations that she wasn't familiar with herself. Several chapters of *Persuasion* are set in Lyme Regis, in Dorset. This was an affordable option, 'frequented', according to a contemporary guidebook, 'principally by persons in the middle class of life'. The Austens had visited it in part because of its affordability, and Captain Wentworth's friend Captain Harville, who is injured and on sick pay, has clearly selected it for the same reason. Lyme Regis was far less magnificent than somewhere like Brighton. Austen, while extolling the beauty of the surrounding cliffs and countryside, admits that 'there is nothing to admire in the buildings themselves'.

SHIP
TAVERN

The town was considered remarkable chiefly for its high, curving harbour wall, the Cobb. It's possible to walk along it, and Austen has a character jump from it, severely injuring herself in an attempt to demonstrate the decisiveness and strength of mind that Captain Wentworth claims to admire.

Opposite Benjamin John Merifield Donne, *Mary Anning*, 1850. Possibly from an earlier portrait.

Above Lyme Regis's harbour wall, the Cobb, prominently featured in *Persuasion*.

You do sometimes see visitors re-enacting this scene from *Persuasion*, but Lyme Regis is better known nowadays as the home of the self-educated nineteenth-century palaeontologist Mary Anning, whose extraordinary discoveries ought to have made her much more famous, far sooner. Mary was about five when, in the autumn of 1804, the Austens visited Lyme Regis, but Jane did encounter her father, Richard Anning, and mentions him in a letter. He worked as a carpenter – which is the capacity in which Jane seems to refer to him – but he also sold fossils to tourists: samples of the ammonites and belemnites and gryphaea that appear in their thousands along the Dorset coast as the soft rock of the cliffs erodes. Occasionally, as happened in 1811, larger and more impressive fossilized remains are revealed.

Fossils

Towards the end of Jane Austen's life there was a sudden spike in interest in fossils, as it became widely recognized that rather than being the devil's toenails, or snakes turned to stone by mediaeval saints, they were in fact the remains of extinct prehistoric animals, and of plant life too; all that was left to tell of a former world. So many large fossils were excavated at Lyme Regis – several by the young Mary Anning and her brother Joseph – that a 'fossil repository' was set up in the town to house them. The public could also visit Bullock's Museum in Piccadilly, in London, a natural history collection which included, among an eclectic mix of exhibits, a number of fossils, both from Britain and further afield. Advertisements for the museum appeared in newspapers across the British Isles in 1814 and 1815, making particular mention of a mammoth and of an 'enormous Crocodile lately found entire in the cliff near Lyme' – in fact an ichthyosaur. The effect on a population where many had been raised to believe in the literal truth of the Biblical Creation must have been deeply unsettling.

Below Thomas Hosmer Shepherd, *Bullock's Museum, 22 Piccadilly*, 1810.

Right *Megatherium and Human Skeletons*, c.1822. During the first quarter of the 19th century, fossil discoveries were challenging traditional beliefs.

Another seaside resort we know Jane visited is Worthing, in Sussex, about ten miles westwards along the coast from Brighton. This was more expensive and select than Lyme Regis, boasting a large, flat, sandy beach. Worthing has been put forward as the model for Sanditon, the main setting in the novel Austen was working on in 1816–7, shortly before she died. Both are situated on the coast of Sussex, though Sanditon is clearly much smaller and newer. Tom Parker, a prime mover in the project, calls it '"a young and rising Bathing-place"', and contrasts it with '"your large, overgrown Places like Brighton, or Worthing, or East Bourne"' [sic]. Worthing had developed very rapidly, particularly after it played host to George III's youngest daughter, Princess Amelia, in 1798. Within living memory it had been little more than a small fishing village and it seems likely that this history of quick expansion and abrupt social change may well have helped to inspire Austen's story.

Austen's final work amounts to about fifty or sixty pages of text in a modern edition, somewhere between a quarter and a sixth of a novel. It is possible that we haven't yet encountered all of the principal characters (Wickham, for example, appears a little later on in *Pride and Prejudice*), and it's also possible that not all of the story was intended to take place at the seaside. Frequently seen as a new departure for Austen, or an anticipation of the meaty 'state of the nation' novels that would appear later in the nineteenth century, *Sanditon* does feel different, perhaps more modern. It must be set more or less at the point when it was written, because one character refers to Waterloo, the decisive battle in the summer of 1815 in which Napoleon Bonaparte was finally and comprehensively defeated. Early on, the character who is usually thought the most likely to become Austen's heroine, Charlotte Heywood, leaves the security of her old-fashioned rural home behind. As it stands, the story combines three strands: friction between new ways and old, and between the middle and upper classes; 'speculation' – risky investment – close to home for Austen, given the collapse of her brother Henry's bank the previous year; and, perhaps surprisingly given that she herself was very unwell at the time of writing, health and hypochondria.

Sanditon

Jane's last, unfinished novel was not a secret to her family. They had two copies of it – the author's own manuscript and another seemingly written out by Cassandra. They must have talked about it, because they seemed confident it was at one point going to be called *The Brothers*. One niece even played around with the text and we have her extended, though still unfinished, version.

The existence of the fragment was revealed to the rest of the world in 1871, when a summary of its contents was included in the memoir published by Jane's nephew. It attracted little attention. One popular, early twentieth-century biography of Jane doesn't even mention it. In 1925, however, the fragment was published by Oxford University Press, to rather more fanfare and newspaper column inches than books from academic presses commonly receive. The editor was Robert William Chapman (see page 162), who would become a prominent figure in Austen studies and, in true scholarly style, since we don't know for sure how the author herself referred to the work, the title page called it *Fragment of a Novel*. On the front cover, however, was the name by which it has been known ever since: *Sanditon*.

The recent television adaptation, having quickly lost sight of the original text, eventually ran to three seasons, but there were plenty of earlier attempts to finish the story. In 1948 the BBC ran a competition offering 40 guineas to the person who came up with the best ending as judged by a panel of experts, and the first continuation had appeared fifteen years earlier than that, in 1932. Written by Alice Cobbett, this was titled *Somehow Lengthened* (you'll occasionally see it referred to as *Somewhat Lengthened*). Reviews weren't bad, though several suggested the additions were too melodramatic, with its smugglers and the kidnapping of one of the main characters, Cobbett's book bears in places a strong resemblance to Georgette Heyer, who, though she was yet to start writing her popular Regency romances, had already published several set during the eighteenth century.

Until the television series came along, the best-known completion of the story was one published in 1975, advertised as being written by Jane Austen and 'another lady'. This topped *The Sunday Times* bestseller list and also sold extremely well in the United States. Interest was piqued by its appearing so close to the 200th anniversary of Jane Austen's birth, as well as by the author's anonymity (she was later revealed as Marie Dobbs, the Australian-born wife of a British diplomat, already published under different pen names). Though, again, the influence of Heyer is readily discernible, Dobbs was a competent author and provided readers with something recognizable and familiar.

More authors experimented with *Sanditon* after Austen's popularity surged in the 1990s. Most showed greater enthusiasm than skill and the problem they all encountered is that there is simultaneously too much of the original text and not enough of it. At times Austen is prolix – something you could almost never accuse her of in her published work. Pages are given over to the three tediously hypochondriac Parker siblings and to detailing the thoughts and impressions of Charlotte Heywood, the probable heroine. Meanwhile, other characters are only faintly sketched and the fragment breaks off just as we encounter the two who seem to promise the most interest, Miss Lambe and the 'very good looking' Mr Sidney Parker.

The detective novelist Reginald Hill published an instalment in his long-running series which was called *A Cure for All Diseases* (published as *The Price of Butcher's Meat* in North America). This saw his gruff policeman hero, Andy Dalziel, team up with psychologist Charley Heywood to solve a murder in a health resort called Sandytown. Hill used the device of having Charley write emails to a sister, describing the people she meets, tracking Austen fairly closely. Readers complained that the emails were too long and took up far too much room. The multimedia drama *Welcome to Sanditon* tried replacing Charlotte with a character of its own invention – not completely successfully, though the show remains worth watching.

Donald Measham's *Jane Austen Out of The Blue* took yet another approach: adding even more material. It introduces multiple characters from other Austen novels, imagining how life might have panned out after their respective happy endings. The result is long, dense, metafictional and, in places, odd. Odder still is Helen Marshall's contemporary short story *Sanditon*, where a young woman extracts the novel from under her own skin.

You can find some supporting evidence for everything from a Heyeresque abduction to body horror in Austen's text if you look hard enough, but each continuation belongs more to the period in which it was finished than the one in which the original fragment was begun. We can't tell what Austen would have ended up doing with the text, nor what she might have gone on to do. She was forty-one when she died, an age at which many novelists are only just getting into their stride. Charles Dickens produced *Bleak House*, *A Tale of Two Cities* and *Great Expectations* in his forties. George Eliot didn't start writing *Middlemarch* until she was fifty-one. There is a whole world of potential stories that Austen might have written, and didn't get the chance to.

Opposite A promotional image for the television adaptation of *Sanditon*, 2019–2023.

Opposite William Heath, *Mermaids at Brighton*, 1825–30. Men often swam naked in the sea, but women generally wore more modest attire.

The seaside resorts were to some extent in competition with spa towns: sea bathing and sea air were sold as health-giving rather than fun. If you ventured into the sea, you usually did so – especially if you were female – in a bathing machine, a sort of caravan in which you changed your clothes before being taken out to a reasonable depth. You would often be accompanied by a 'dipper' to encourage you or, in some cases, dunk you in the water. Dippers were probably also a wise safety precaution, since the bather was sometimes concealed from sight by an awning, and an ability to swim strongly was not common at this point. The process doesn't sound enjoyable and some resorts offered visitors purpose-built bath houses which were supplied with warm sea water as well as cold.

Medical advisers might recommend courses of treatment at particular seaside resorts, just as they did at spas and, as happened with spa towns, amenities and service industries sprang up to provide for – and exploit – the influx of visitors. *Sanditon* begins with entrepreneurial Tom Parker having a carriage accident while trying to find a doctor who can be tempted to move to the coast, thus making the new resort more desirable to visitors. His business partner, Lady Denham, keeps 'asses' (donkeys) and is ever hopeful that visitors might be prescribed their milk, which was considered restorative. Tom Parker's sisters and younger brother are prepared to take extreme and expensive measures to treat their imagined ill-health: having teeth removed, drinking various types of 'Herb-Tea' and consulting '"Physician after Physician"'. Medical care of all kinds was a lucrative business and entire local economies became dependent on it.

"'A little sea-bathing would set me up forever.'"

Pride and Prejudice

Below Thomas Rowlandson, *The Hypochondriac*, 1788, after J. Dunthorne. In her final piece of fiction, now known as *Sanditon*, Jane pokes fun at a set of siblings who needlessly agonize about their health.

Opposite William Maddocks, *Sake Dean Mahomed*, 1822. Mahomed set up Britain's first Indian restaurant and the 'Turkish Baths' in Brighton.

The one character in *Sanditon* who appears to be in genuinely delicate health is Miss Lambe. The manuscript breaks off before we meet her properly, and we never get to hear her say anything or interact with anybody. This is especially frustrating because she is the only biracial character in Austen's fiction.

Britain was not as ethnically homogeneous during Austen's lifetime as some people imagine. There had been a Romani presence in the country for hundreds of years. Most large towns, and almost all dock towns, had fairly sizeable Jewish populations (see pages 116–7). Protestant religious refugees had been arriving from France since the sixteenth century and when the French revolution broke out, political refugees followed them. Tom Lefroy, with whom Jane is supposed to have fallen in love, had, as his surname suggests, French roots. There was already a steady flow of immigration into Britain from Ireland.

At Brighton, there was a Turkish bath run by a man called Sake Dean Mahomed. There are quite frequent references in newspapers to 'Turks' and 'Mussulmen' [sic], and also to 'Lascars' – a blanket term used to describe sailors originating from around the Indian Ocean, and occasionally applied to those from further afield. There are also references to men and women 'of colour'. Attitudes to interracial relationships were relatively relaxed at this point, especially among the British communities living in India, and there were not insignificant numbers of people in the British Isles who had dual heritage.

It's impossible to tell what Austen was planning to do with Miss Lambe. We don't have any idea how sensitively she would have dealt with the issue of race. We don't even know for certain whether the character's West Indian background would have ended up being prominent in the finished story.

Look in the background of some of the contemporary seaside pictures, though, and you can just discern larger vessels out in the deeper water or on the horizon: warships or merchantmen heading back home after visiting foreign ports. Britain's interests extended globally – and so too did Austen's.

Empire and Slavery

"'[...] a delightful voyage to Bengal or Barbadoes [...]'"

The foolish Camilla Stanley
in the early fragment *Catherine, or the Bower*

In the late 1860s one of Jane Austen's many nephews published a memoir about her. In some ways it is as interesting for what it leaves out as for what it includes. Jane's brother George and uncle Thomas are made to vanish. We learn a lot about Jane's mother's family, the Leighs, and about more distant maternal relatives such as the Brydges. But the author is tight-lipped on the subject of Jane's father's family, not even mentioning the names of her paternal grandparents. We saw that there may have been question marks over the marriage of William Austen and Rebecca Walter (née Hampson); he had only been a surgeon but Rebecca's father had inherited a baronetcy, which was passed on to her brother. Rebecca's sisters all married men who were comfortably situated, or even rich. One did ally herself first to a Mr Smith, which might recall Sir Walter Elliot's snobbish outburst in *Persuasion* ("'– a mere Mrs Smith, an every day Mrs Smith, of all people and all names in the world [...]'"), but later redeemed matters by marrying a man surnamed Cure. Another was a bedchamber attendant to George III's mother.

Leaving them out of the memoir seems, on the surface, an odd decision. These people – the Hampsons and Freemans, the Cures and the Paynes – were, after all, Jane's great-aunts and great-uncles, and though she didn't know them herself, she was on visiting terms with several of their children and grandchildren. This side of the family had titles, land and lots of money, but they may well have been considered an embarrassment by the 1860s, because their fortunes and their estates had been funded, in part, by slave labour in the West Indies.

Opposite Detail from a view of a sugar plantation in Jamaica, colourized engraving from *L'album, giornale letterario e di belle arti,* Saturday, September 9, 1837, Year 4. A number of Austen's relatives owned property on the island.

"'William must not forget my shawl if he goes to the East Indies; and I shall give him a commission for anything else that is worth having.'"

Mansfield Park

There's been a certain amount of resistance over the years to suggestions that we should think about Jane Austen in the context of slavery and empire. But the forts of Bengal and the sugar plantations of the Caribbean were really not that far removed from her.

Jane's aunt Philadelphia had gone out to India to be married; Jane's cousin Eliza had been born in what was then known as Calcutta. Their money was Indian money; they brought Indian servants back to Britain with them. Frank and Charles Austen travelled all over the world during their long naval careers, including to both the East and West Indies. In 1808 Frank received a gift from the East India Company after escorting one of their convoys of merchant ships. Charles is buried in Trincomalee, in Sri Lanka, having died of cholera while heading British naval forces during the second Anglo-Burmese War.

Charles's first wife, Frances Palmer, was the daughter of the Attorney General of Bermuda, as was his second, Frances's sister Harriet (marriage between a man and his sister-in-law was legal). James Austen married Anne Mathew, whose father owned property and enslaved individuals in Dominica. Cassandra Austen's fiancé, Tom Fowle, went to the West Indies as a chaplain for his relation, Lord Craven, and died near San Domingo in February 1797. Aunt Leigh Perrot had been born in Barbados and inherited a substantial amount of money derived from Barbadian property. One of the Reverend George Austen's nephews bought an estate in Jamaica. Several of his other relations also owned land in Jamaica or had financial interests there. For the avoidance of doubt, in their wills they refer to people on those properties who were enslaved.

You cannot, of course, choose your family, or the families that your relations marry into, but according to recent research by Azar Hussein, at least one Hampson family connection was sent to be educated at the school at Steventon. The Reverend Austen made one of his slave-owning cousins, a man called John Cope Freeman, godfather to his youngest son Charles. He maintained a long-standing friendship with James Nibbs, who owned property in Antigua, agreeing to act as a trustee if required and accepting his son as a pupil. Nibbs was also godfather – and namesake – to the eldest of Jane's brothers, James.

Jane isn't responsible for what her in-laws, or cousins or aunts and uncles, or even her father did. But she did know a number of these people socially; she accepted hospitality and presents from them, she loved some of them. A portion of her father's income came from the bank accounts of men who deemed it acceptable to visit appalling cruelties on people, in pursuit of profit. She was, occasionally, a guest in houses which had been partly financed by profound suffering. To a degree, she is implicated.

Very few people in Britain *weren't* implicated, though, one way or another. Jane Austen lived in what was rapidly becoming a global economy. If you drank tea, or ate sugar or spices, or wore cotton; if you knocked back the daily ration of rum which was handed out in the Royal Navy, treated your toothache with laudanum, or held any kind of investment or annuity, then you probably couldn't consider yourself untouched by the horrors of slavery or the corrupt business practices (and worse) of the East India Company.

The idea that it is possible to be guilty by association, to be morally contaminated by what happens thousands of miles away, wouldn't have been an unfamiliar one to Austen. Anti-slavery activists brought cases in the English law courts and published

Below Stephen Slaughter, *Sir George Hampson and Family*, c.1738. Sir George was Jane Austen's great-uncle and, like others in that branch of the family, owned property in Jamaica.

Below Title page of one of several abolitionist texts published by Thomas Clarkson, 1789.

Opposite *Shah Allum, Mogul of Hindostan, reviewing the East India Company's troops*, perhaps by Tilly Kettle, 1781. The brief reign of Shah Alam I ushered in a period of instability leading to the decline of the Mughal empire.

poems and pamphlets in which they talked about the conditions under which the sugar on British tea tables had been produced. In the 1790s, there was a consumer boycott of West Indian products. And one governor-general of India, Warren Hastings, was tried in the Houses of Parliament for corruption and abuses allegedly committed overseas.

The Mughal dynasty had ruled over the Indian subcontinent for 200 years, from the early 1500s, and had permitted the establishment of several European trading posts within its territories. From the 1720s, however, the power of the Mughals began to decline. With the succession insecure, independence movements arose within the empire, and invasion threatened from without. The better-established Dutch, Portuguese, French and British trading consortia began jockeying to secure their own positions and crowd out any newcomers. They were, by the middle of the eighteenth century, large and powerful companies with considerable financial reserves, subject to scant oversight or control from their respective governments. The duties on imports were large enough to discourage too many searching questions. Through the 1760s and 1770s the British East India Company and its rivals expanded their security teams into private armies and even hired extra soldiers from regular regiments. They sought to win the favour of the rulers of the many Indian kingdoms, waging wars and pocketing bribes, skimming off taxes and interfering in politics.

Active in the British East India Company during this period was Warren Hastings. As was common, he had joined them when he was still a teenager, sinking his resources into obtaining a 'writership', a junior position in the company. Hastings, the impecunious son of an Anglican vicar, was typical

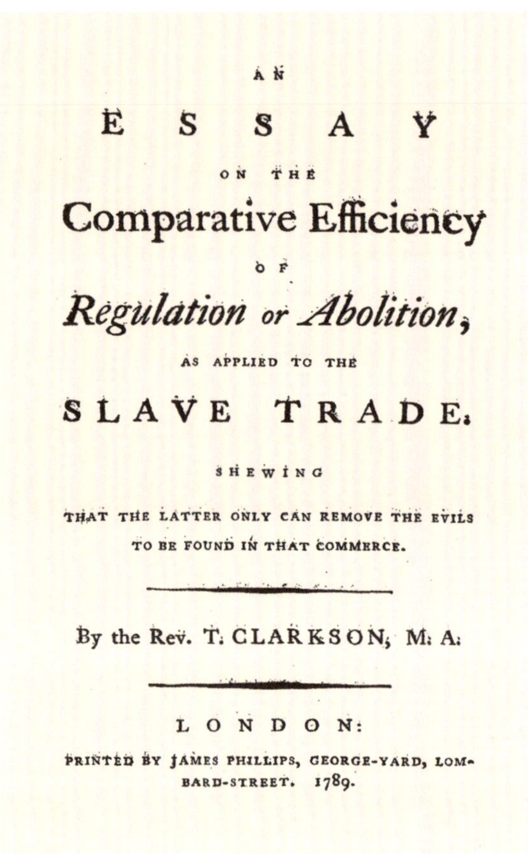
AN

ESSAY

ON THE

Comparative Efficiency

OF

Regulation or Abolition,

AS APPLIED TO THE

SLAVE TRADE.

SHEWING

THAT THE LATTER ONLY CAN REMOVE THE EVILS TO BE FOUND IN THAT COMMERCE.

By the Rev. T. CLARKSON, M. A.

LONDON:

PRINTED BY JAMES PHILLIPS, GEORGE-YARD, LOMBARD-STREET. 1789.

of the kind of young Britons who were attracted to India: just rich enough to fund the voyage out and desperate enough to make it. The journey, passing round the southern tip of Africa, took months, encountering rough seas and extremes of weather. Once they had arrived, many Europeans fell victim to the climate, or to tropical diseases. There were great fortunes to be made, but not safely nor – for the most part – honestly.

Opposite Sir Joshua Reynolds, *Warren Hastings*, 1766–1767. Hastings was godfather to Jane Austen's cousin Eliza.

Above *A view of Fort William in the Kingdom of Bengal*, 1794. Jane Austen's aunt Philadelphia lived in Kolkata for many years and it was where her cousin Eliza was born.

Nevertheless, it was not only men who made the trip. In 1752 George Austen's sister, Jane's aunt Philadelphia, had set sail for Madras (Chennai). The following year, she married a man called Tysoe Saul Hancock, a surgeon employed by the Company. The couple settled in Calcutta (Kolkata), where they made the acquaintance of Warren Hastings. He and Mr Hancock became business associates and when, in 1761, the Hancocks had a little girl, called Eliza or Betsy, Hastings was made her godfather. In 1765, after a power struggle, he resigned his position and they all appear to have travelled back to England together. According to eighteenth-century scandalmongers, Hastings and Philadelphia were lovers. It's sometimes suggested that he may have been Eliza's father. He did give Eliza £10,000 – a gift which made a significant difference to her life and marriage prospects. Why he did it, though, whether for love or friendship, or to repay a debt, remains uncertain.

There is also a tradition that Hastings's son was looked after by Jane Austen's parents for some time

Below A portrait recently reidentified as showing Tysoe Saul Hancock, his wife Philadelphia (née Austen), their daughter Eliza and an Indian servant, Clarinda, by Sir Joshua Reynolds, 1765-1767.

early in their marriage, before he died tragically young from what was called the putrid throat (a term which usually indicated diphtheria). It is extremely difficult to track down any corroborating evidence, however. There are no obvious burial records; it's possible the child in question may perhaps have been a step-son, or even illegitimate. But the very fact that the story exists at all suggests that there may have been very strong personal ties between Hastings and the Austens.

Both Hastings and Hancock returned to India to top up their bank accounts. Hancock didn't prosper, dying in 1775, but Hastings became increasingly powerful, and increasingly subject to criticism. He was given the title of governor-general and under his governorship the Company held firm against the Rohillas of Uttar Pradesh, the Marathas and the kingdom of Mysore, as well as the French, and even expanded its zone of influence. However, seeking additional funds, Hastings helped himself to the contents of a royal treasury – only one of several morally (and legally) questionable decisions that would later return to haunt him.

Early in 1786, Hastings was impeached – charged with misconduct in office. The prime movers against him were the radical politician Charles James Fox and, perhaps unexpectedly, Edmund Burke. The fact that Burke's *Reflections on the Revolution in France* is a conservative text isn't really up for debate, but many of his tendencies were more liberal. The corruption and greed displayed by the East India Company offended his idea of the kind of country Britain was and what its influence in the world ought to be.

The problems may have been systemic ones but the impeachment was very personal. It was Hastings who stood accused of lining his own pockets, taking bribes, mistreating women and installing a local ruler who tortured farmers to extort additional money from them. Eliza's baby son was born in the summer of 1786, meaning that although the decision to christen him Hastings, after her godfather, may have been made with an eye to any future inheritance, it was also a public declaration of loyalty. When proceedings began, the opening speeches attracted a large and influential audience, with the trial becoming, for a time, a fashionable place to see and be seen. Interest died away because, in the event, the impeachment lumbered on for nearly a decade, until 1795, when it ended in acquittal, but Hastings's reputation – and that of the East India Company – never fully recovered.

Jane Austen was ten when the impeachment process began, probably too small to understand it properly. By the time of the acquittal, though, she was nearly twenty. Two years later, in 1797, Eliza was transformed from a cousin into a sister-in-law by marrying Henry Austen. Her Indian-sourced money, her former governor-general godfather, and the child she had named after him were all drawn even closer to the Austen family.

Jane first wrote about India in a fragment called *Catherine, or the Bower* – one of the most mature and serious of her teenage pieces, which unlike most of the others seems to have been intended as the beginning of an ambitious, much longer text. In that, one of the heroine's close friends has been sent out to India by her extended family and married off to an uncongenial older man – a plot thread that has to have been at least partly inspired by Aunt Philadelphia's experiences. In *Sense and Sensibility*, Colonel Brandon has served for several years in India, probably in a regular British army regiment hired by the East India Company. The dating of the story is for various reasons a little uncertain, but whenever Austen's early nineteenth-century readers imagined Brandon had been in India, the associations would not have been very positive ones.

Even Willoughby, whose own morals are hardly impeccable, appears disapproving, suggesting sardonically that Brandon's conversation '"[...] may have extended to the existence of nabobs, gold mohrs, and palanquins"'. Nabob (more correctly nawab) was one of several Indian royal titles and also what the British called men who had returned from India with almost certainly ill-gotten fortunes; one of the main charges against Warren Hastings, incidentally, was that he had stolen considerable property from the female relatives of the Nawab of Oudh. A *mohr* or *mohur* was a unit of currency, while palanquins were the large, luxurious litters in which a single passenger reclined in comfort, carried by multiple bearers. One way and another, this all seems quite pointed. Given that *Sense and Sensibility* features a number of fortunes changing hands – often, it's implied, unfairly – we might think that these Indian terms, connected with money and luxury, play on the same theme.

There are a few other passing references to the 'East Indies' in Austen's work: in *Mansfield Park* there's some suggestion that the heroine's naval officer brother might be stationed out there, and another, younger brother is working on an 'Indiaman' – an East India Company merchant ship. Close as East Indian concerns came to the Austens, hotly as they were debated, what was happening in the West Indies touched them even more closely, and aroused greater public anger.

Opposite *A View of the Tryal of Warren Hastings Esqr. before the Court of Peers, in Westminster Hall*, after Edward Dayes, 1789.

Below *Cheyte Sing* [i.e. Chait Singh] *rendering homage to Warren Hastings*, an illustration from a Victorian history book, perhaps suggestive of Hastings's problematic reputation.

Right Detail from the frontispiece of Phillis Wheatley's *Poems on Various Subjects, Religious and Moral*, 1773.

Far right An anti-slavery medallion, one of many distributed by the Wedgwood manufactory from the late 1780s onwards. The words around the edge, which read 'Am I not a man and a brother?', became an abolitionist rallying cry.

Below An illustration from a publication produced by an abolitionist group in Birmingham, England, *c.*1825.

Atlantic slavery was horrific. It was also an international business that involved slave traders from three continents, propped up economies in the Caribbean and Americas, created new markets and drove investment around the world. People were not the only cargo that slave ships transported. After unloading a 'consignment' of African abductees, often prisoners of war, and sometimes simply victims of kidnapping, captains would reload with sugar and tobacco and cotton, and return to European markets where they could sell the products at a premium before taking European-made goods to the west coast of Africa. Then they would pick up more enslaved individuals and repeat the process, over and over again.

Cotton, sugar and tobacco were all labour-intensive crops and if the workforce had been regularly employed – and paid for their efforts – profits would have been limited, perhaps unsustainably so. As it was, even with enslaved and unpaid workers, West Indian plantations were frequently mortgaged and remortgaged or sold in bankruptcy proceedings. Plantations were also often used to supply incomes to daughters and to younger sons, leaving British property intact and unburdened for the heir; the result was that many bankers and lawyers and thousands of families had a personal financial interest in slavery continuing. The practice found active supporters in parliament, in the Church of England and among the landowning classes. It also met with determined and growing opposition.

The abolitionists were an unlikely alliance. Individuals who had been enslaved ranged themselves alongside those who had formerly worked on slave ships and plantations. There were religious non-conformists: evangelicals, Methodists and Quakers who considered slavery contrary to Christian beliefs. There were radical thinkers, some of them, like Thomas Paine and William Godwin, professed atheists. A handful of members of parliament joined the cause, among them people like Charles James Fox, whom we would think of as quite left wing, and the much more conservative William Wilberforce. One of the unlikeliest abolitionists was the Lord Chief Justice, Lord Mansfield, who in the early 1770s essentially declared slavery legally unenforceable in England.

Authors played their part too, with texts by Ignatius Sancho and Phillis Wheatley, the African-American poet, finding a wide audience, as did the memoir of his own experiences written by Olaudah Equiano (also known as Gustavus Vassa). William Cowper published a number of poems attacking slavery, designed to appeal to both the intellectual elite and popular audiences. The medallion produced by the famous Quaker pottery designer Josiah Wedgwood also proved highly effective. It showed a man in chains praying on his knees and the words 'Am I not a man and brother?' and copies were distributed widely. Abolitionists employed every means at their disposal to promote their cause, from simple jingles and woodcuts to consumer boycotts, law cases and parliamentary enquiries.

Partial victory came with the passing of the Abolition of the Slave Trade Act of 1807, which made it illegal for British ships to transport people from the slave markets of West Africa across the Atlantic. It would be another quarter of a century before slavery itself was officially abolished in the majority of British overseas territories, in 1833, and longer still before it actually came to an end, but the crucial battle for hearts and minds was won during Jane Austen's lifetime.

The Somerset case

William Murray, the boy who would go on to become Lord Mansfield, was born into a Scottish family with pro-Stuart sympathies. He left Scotland – and Jacobitism – behind as a teenager, and after being educated at Westminster School, and at Christ Church, Oxford, he pursued a legal and political career, with great success. He was a member of the Privy Council and served at various times as solicitor general, attorney general and, on occasion, lord chancellor and speaker of the House of Lords. He also rose to the office of Lord Chief Justice.

In 1772 Mansfield was asked to decide, in essence, whether a man called James Somerset could be forcibly returned to Virginia by Charles Stewart, the man who claimed to own him, or whether this was a case of kidnapping, an illegal abduction. Somerset had been brought to Britain by Stewart three years earlier. He had run away and succeeded in remaining free for some time but was unfortunate enough to be spotted by members of Stewart's household on a London street, seized and bundled aboard a ship. Campaigners brought a case against Stewart on his behalf, a writ of habeas corpus. This was a long-standing article of English law designed to prevent arbitrary detention, but there were exceptions to it: men could, for example, legally confine their wives.

The legal situation with regard to slavery in England was complex. Serfdom had almost entirely vanished. Other forms of bonded labour did still exist, but were on the way out. In the earlier decades of the eighteenth century enslaved people who had escaped in Britain had sometimes been formally released by the courts, and sometimes returned to their 'owners'. An early edition of one of the most influential legal text books of the period, William Blackstone's *Commentaries on the Laws of England*, declared that 'liberty is [...] rooted even in our very soil' and that anyone arriving in the country became free 'eo instanti' [that very moment], whatever their status in other jurisdictions. Blackstone grew uneasy about this passage being quoted, however, and altered it in later editions, though he continued to insist that anyone in England 'falls under the protection of the laws'.

Lord Mansfield was one of the most senior judges in the country. What he decided in this case would – probably, arguably – be binding precedent for all lower courts, at least until parliament chose to get involved. It would certainly be cited in any future cases.

He was under a lot of pressure. The pro-slavery lobby was large, rich and powerful, and he had already made an enemy of them with his judgement in the Hylas case of 1768, where he had declared that a husband's right to his wife trumped that of her master, regardless of ethnicity. But John Hylas had been manumitted (formally freed) and English law was at this point very clear that man and wife were one legal person. Whatever Mansfield decided, the case of Somerset was likely to have much wider repercussions.

Since the Somerset case predates the era of reliable law reporting, we don't know exactly how Lord Mansfield's judgement was worded. But there are several contemporary or near-contemporary documents that purport to record it and it's likely that it was actually quite dry and technical. Mansfield seems to have made a point of stating that contracts around enslaved people were legally valid, but that the people themselves nevertheless still had rights and legal protections, and *that* was what the case centred on. Stewart couldn't keep Somerset on the ship – or any ship – against his will. As critics of the judgement were quick to point out, the two statements were mutually pretty inconsistent but this does seem to have been an accurate statement of the legal position, and Blackstone arrived independently at a similar one at around the same time.

One source suggests that Mansfield used a phrase sometimes employed by judges who know that they are about to cause chaos but see no alternative: *fiat iustitia, ruat caelum* – let there be justice, there must be justice whatever the cost, though the heavens fall.

One of Mansfield's later judgements, in the case of the ship Zong, was seen as a failure for abolitionists – the deaths of dozens of enslaved people, deliberately thrown overboard, were discussed only in the context of fraud rather than murder. He had already struck a powerful blow against slavery, however, casting its legality – and its future – into serious doubt not just in England, but much further afield.

Opposite James Hallyer, *Granville Sharp the Abolitionist Rescuing a Slave from the Hands of His Master*, 1864. The enslaved man depicted here was called Jonathan Strong. The case was another early legal victory for the abolitionist cause.

Left Lemuel Francis Abbott, *William Cowper*, 1792. Jane Austen appears to have been a great admirer of Cowper and mentions or quotes from him several times.

Jane knew a number of people who owned or had owned slaves. Several of them were her own relatives, others connections by marriage. But whereas her disapproval of the East India Company has to be inferred, her attitudes towards the subject of slavery seem much clearer. In one letter she professes her admiration for the abolitionist activist and author Thomas Clarkson and she quotes the anti-slavery poet William Cowper on several occasions in her fiction; for many readers this would have been understood as a declaration of where her sympathies lay.

At one point in *Emma* the well-educated, thoughtful Jane Fairfax talks about the governess career which awaits her, mentioning the agencies in London which arrange the ‘“sale – not quite of human flesh – but of human intellect”’. The appalling Mrs Elton leaps in, imagining that ‘“a fling at the slave-trade”’ is implied. She is, we've been told, from Bristol, a town which had grown rich on the back of that trade, making her defensiveness rather suggestive. Jane Fairfax, who is in general very cautious about what she says, protests that she ‘“was not thinking of the slave-trade”’, only ‘“governess-trade”’, but goes on to refer to ‘“the guilt of those who carry it on”’ and the ‘“misery of the victims”’ before she regains control of herself. We might not nowadays agree with her attempt to compare working as a private tutor – however uncongenial – to being enslaved, but her moral disgust is very obvious. Nor is she the only quiet and cautious character to bring up the slave trade. Fanny Price does so too, in *Mansfield Park*.

Commentators disagree on whether *Mansfield Park* is 'about' slavery or not. On the one hand, Fanny says that she ‘“love[s] to hear my uncle talk of the West Indies”’, that it ‘“entertains”’ her, which hardly sounds overtly disapproving. We never learn exactly what it is she asks about the slave trade, or why it should have been met with ‘“such a dead silence”’.

On the other hand, Fanny is made to quote William Cowper and there are a significant number of other literary references in the novel – prose, poems, plays – which circle around the subject of slavery, several of which were very well known at the time. And Austen was personally acquainted with the family of Lord Mansfield.

Austen also chose to name a deeply unpleasant character 'Mrs Norris'. One real-life Mr Norris, Robert Norris, was a notorious pro-slavery campaigner; another, the Reverend Henry Handley Norris, was prominent in several Church of England committees and organizations, including the Society for the Propagation of the Gospel, which ran its own slave plantation in the Caribbean. Henry Handley Norris was

The Mansfield connection

Lord Mansfield and his wife took several young relatives to live in their household. Among them were the two girls in this portrait, both great-nieces: Elizabeth Murray, whose mother had been a German aristocrat, and Dido, the illegitimate daughter of Mansfield's nephew John Lindsay, a naval officer, and a Black woman named Maria Bell or Belle.

Though lovely in its way, the picture isn't unproblematic. Dido is exoticized and is on her feet while her cousin sits and reads. The evidence as to how she was treated by her father's family is contradictory. She seems to have been given a decent education but as an adult was kept in the background; she received several modest bequests from older relations but the witnesses at her wedding were servants. If we see affection between the cousins in the portrait, however, that may not be wishful thinking. There was considerable difference in their social status but the two girls did spend a lot of time together.

The link to Austen comes because when Elizabeth Murray got married, to George Finch-Hatton (a relative of her great-aunt, Mansfield's wife), she moved to Kent and in later years she became well acquainted with Edward Austen and his family. Jane met her on at least four occasions that we know of, though she was unimpressed, complaining in a letter that Lady Elizabeth had 'astonishingly little to say for herself', especially for 'a woman of her age & situation'. This comment seems to indicate that Jane had expected better and thus presumably knew something of the older woman's background. We can't be sure whether that extended to knowing about Dido, but there can be little doubt that she would have been aware of the link to Lord Mansfield.

Below Cousins Dido Belle and Elizabeth Murray, great nieces of Lord Mansfield, c.1776. Jane Austen was acquainted with the latter.

"'Did not you hear me ask [...] about the slave trade last night?' 'I did, and was in hopes the question would be followed up by others [...]' 'And I longed to do it – but there was such a dead silence!'" Mansfield Park

Opposite *William Murray, 1st Earl of Mansfield, 1705-1793, Lord Chief Justice*, after David Martin, c.1770s. Many people believed that Mansfield had effectively outlawed slavery in England.

Charles Austen's letter

In the special collections of the Bodleian Library in Oxford you can find a box containing some of Henry Handley Norris's papers. Among them is a letter addressed to Norris. It was written by Christopher Wordsworth, a clergyman and academic, younger brother of the poet William Wordsworth, and in it he mentions having intercepted a letter from 'Captain Austin R.N. of his Majesty's ship Namur'. That's Charles Austen, Jane's younger brother. The *Namur* was an old ship and during Charles's captaincy of her, she was docked at the Nore, the sandbank anchorage in the Thames Estuary, off Sheerness. The *Namur* also served as the flagship for Admiral Sir Thomas Williams, who had been married to the Austens' cousin Jane Cooper and helped both Charles and Francis Austen in their naval careers.

Christopher Wordsworth was deeply conservative, particularly on church matters. Other letters to Norris refer to their dislike of the Bible Society, a rival to the Anglican Society for the Promotion of Christian Knowledge. This was not, so far as we're aware, a topic that interested Charles much. It's Frank who had the reputation of being religious. But Edward Cooper – Jane Cooper's brother – was very much involved in the Bible Society and this might have been sufficient to bring both his cousin and his brother-in-law under suspicion.

We don't know who Charles's letter was addressed to, nor what it contained, only that it was presumably written (like Wordsworth's letter) in the early autumn of 1813. The episode reminds us, however, that establishment anxieties about political dissent continued for many years after the French Revolution. And it raises intriguing questions about the politics of Jane's family.

also at one point involved in intercepting Charles Austen's mail.

Towards the end of *Persuasion* we're told that the hero, Captain Wentworth, helps Mrs Smith, the heroine's old school friend, to recover 'her husband's estate in the West Indies'. It's one of several apparently unconnected references to the West Indies that appear in the text. Jane might, of course, have either removed them or made much more of them, had she been well enough to extend the novel to a more usual length and revise it to her satisfaction. As it stands, though, the contrast with *Mansfield Park*, and its dense web of cultural allusions, is marked.

But however undeveloped the references are in *Persuasion*, the fact that they are there means that of the six novels and two fragments that Jane left us with, only three manage to avoid mentioning either the East or West Indies, or the slave trade. And even those three use the word 'slave' – negatively – or mention products from territory that Britain already owned or was in the process of taking over: tea, coffee, muslins. These products, these places, these problematic issues were absolutely part of her world, and of the worlds she created in her fiction.

IN
THIS HOUSE
JANE AUSTEN
LIVED HER LAST DAYS
AND DIED

Legacies

"'A valuable legacy indeed!'"

Sense and Sensibility

Jane Austen died soon after sunrise on Friday, 18 July 1817. She was only forty-one but had been unwell since the beginning of the previous year. We remain uncertain what was wrong with her. The most popular, though still unconfirmed, theory is that it was an adrenal disorder: Addison's disease, as was first suggested in the 1960s, though this rests chiefly on a reference Jane makes in a letter of March 1817 to being 'every wrong colour'. There was also a family history of cancer and of bowel problems, both of which can, under certain circumstances, lead to skin discolouration.

A visit to the spa at Cheltenham in the spring of 1816 proved of little benefit. In April 1817 Jane wrote her will, though she neglected to have it witnessed. For the two months prior to her death she had been staying with her sister in Winchester, near a doctor favoured by the family, but in the end neither his skill nor Cassandra's ever-hopeful care was enough to save her. Her final literary composition was a comic poem about the weather, but she also left behind about £800, a few pieces of jewellery, four published novels, two more or less complete manuscripts, her unfinished and early works – and a number of problems for her family.

One problem that was fairly easy to solve was her will. Being unwitnessed, this had to be publicly sworn to. The two individuals who undertook this task were Charles Austen's father-in-law John Grove Palmer and sister-in-law Harriet, who signed the official documents declaring that they were familiar with Jane's 'manner and character of handwriting' and with her signature. The executor and chief beneficiary of the will was Cassandra, but there was a legacy of £50 for Henry – acknowledgement either of the help he had given Jane in her writing career or of his current penurious position, after his bank collapsed, or of both.

Opposite Reputedly, this is the house in College Street in Winchester where Jane Austen was staying when she died.

Right Jane Austen's gravestone, in Winchester Cathedral. Though the inscription is lengthy, it makes no mention of her authorship, only mentioning, 'the extraordinary endowments of her mind'.

Below The title page of the first edition of *Northanger Abbey* and *Persuasion*, published together after Austen's death.

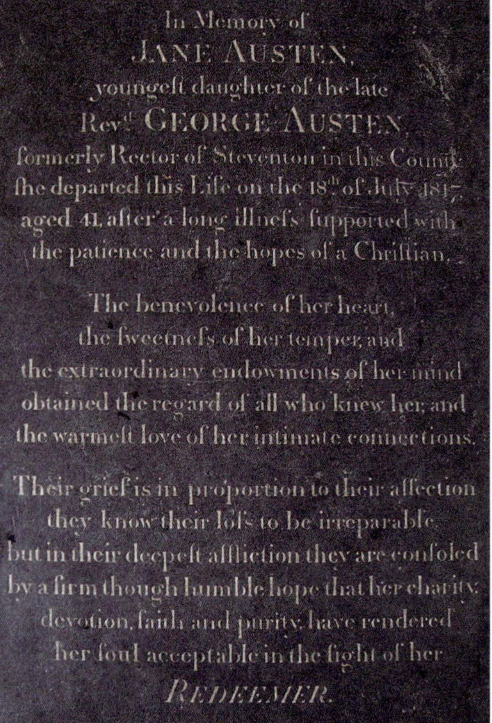

The one remaining legacy, also of £50, was to Madame Bigeon, who had for many years worked for Cousin Eliza. A quarter of a century later, Cassandra would leave Madame Bigeon's daughter Mary Perigord an annuity in her will; there appears to have been an enduring sense either of obligation or affection.

Another problem, or set of problems, was to do with Jane herself: how she ought to be remembered, what to do with her work. Here it seems there may have been disagreement. Famously, the lengthy epitaph on Jane's large and expensive gravestone in Winchester Cathedral includes no reference at all to her writing, though it does mention the 'extraordinary endowments of her mind'. Someone, however, took the decision to post a death notice in the *London Courier and Evening Gazette* identifying her as 'Authoress of *Emma*, *Mansfield Park*, *Pride and Prejudice*, and *Sense and Sensibility*' – the first time her authorship had been publicly acknowledged in print. And by September 1817, Jane's publisher John Murray was writing to Lord Byron, mentioning 'Miss Austen' as 'the ingenious Author of Pride & Prejudice' and announcing that he was going to publish 'Two new Novels left by her'. These were *Northanger Abbey* and *Persuasion*, which went to press at the end of the year, prefaced with a 'Biographical Notice of the Author' usually assumed to have been written by Henry Austen.

The Jane who appears in the Notice is what she herself might have mockingly termed a 'picture of perfection'. We're told that her stature was 'that of true elegance', her 'complexion [...] of the finest texture', her voice 'extremely sweet'. The writer asserts that Jane 'never deserved disapprobation' and that she 'never uttered either a hasty, a silly, or a severe expression'. It's hard not to wonder what she would have felt about it, and, for that matter, what she would have felt about

NORTHANGER ABBEY:

AND

PERSUASION.

BY THE AUTHOR OF "PRIDE AND PREJUDICE," "MANSFIELD-PARK," &c.

WITH A BIOGRAPHICAL NOTICE OF THE AUTHOR.

IN FOUR VOLUMES.

VOL. I.

LONDON:

JOHN MURRAY, ALBEMARLE-STREET.

1818.

Jane's last work

When Winchester races first took
their beginning
It is said the good people forgot their old Saint
Not applying at all for the leave of Saint Swithin
And that William of Wykeham's approval
was faint.

The races however were fixed and determined
The company came and the Weather
was charming
The Lords and the Ladies were satine'd
and ermined
And nobody saw any future alarming. –

But when the old Saint was informed of
these doings
He made but one Spring from his Shrine to
the Roof
Of the Palace which now lies so sadly in ruins
And then he addressed them all standing aloof.

'Oh! Subjects rebellious! Oh Venta depraved
When once we are buried you think we
are gone
But behold me immortal! By vice
you're enslaved
You have sinned and must suffer, then
farther he said

These races and revels and dissolute measures
With which you're debasing a neighboring Plain
Let them stand – You shall meet with your
curse in your pleasures
Set off for your course, I'll pursue with my rain.

Ye cannot but know my command o'er July
Henceforward I'll triumph in shewing
my powers
Shift your race as you will it shall never be dry
The curse upon Venta is July in showers.

Northanger Abbey and *Persuasion* being published, since so far as we can tell the decision to do so was not her own. But her writing – like her reputation – was out of her control now. Over the years that followed, both would gradually move out of her family's control too.

It is sometimes suggested that in the 1820s Austen's novels came close to vanishing into obscurity, and that they were only rescued by Cassandra's decision in 1832 to sell the five copyrights she held to the publisher Richard Bentley (he also obtained the rights to *Pride and Prejudice*, which Jane had sold to Egerton). This doesn't seem to be quite accurate.

The 1820s wasn't a decade when Austen's novels sold in large numbers, but she was being read around the world. She had already been translated into French and pirated in the United States (there was at that point no international copyright). *Northanger Abbey* and *Persuasion* were available to buy in India. Critics and reviewers mentioned 'Miss Austen' fairly frequently, and almost always not just favourably but also as a gold standard that other writers fell short of. More significantly, publishers started comparing other authors to her in newspaper advertisements, something that continued all through the 1820s and early 1830s and beyond.

She wasn't just critically admired; she was known about. Her name was mentioned in a sprightly poem that appeared in the press in 1821. In 1823, a Barbados-based newspaper, *The Barbadian*, printed a long list of recommended topics of 'elegant literary conversation' which included 'Miss Austin – Captain Wentworth – [...]

'[...] charming even as were the works of all her imitators [...]'

Northanger Abbey

Below An early French edition of *L'Abbaye de Northanger* (1824).

Early translations and pirated copies

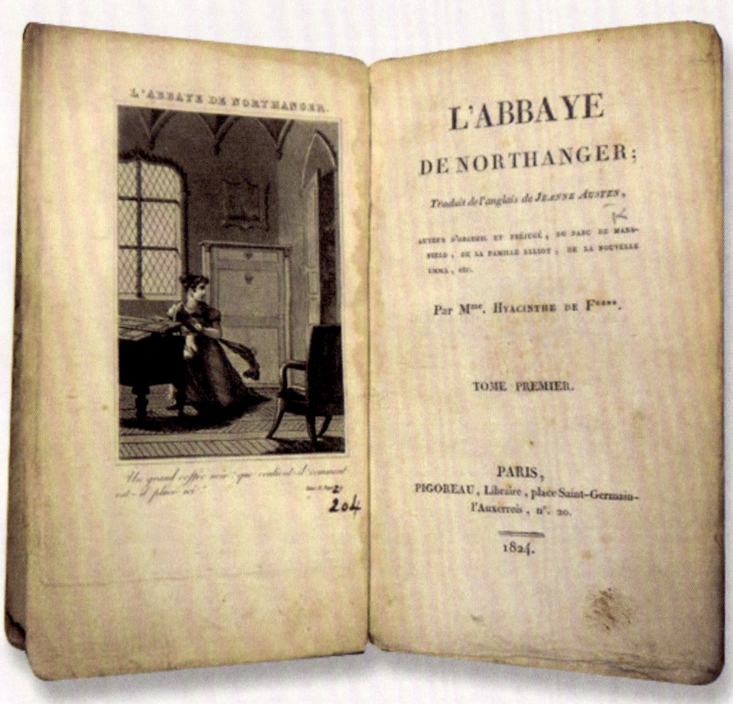

Raison et Sensibilité, an unauthorized and in places loose translation of *Sense and Sensibility* was published in France in 1815. The following year both *La Nouvelle Emma* and *Le Parc de Mansfield* appeared. Together with *La Famille Elliot* (*Persuasion*), *Orgueil et Préjugés* (*Pride and Prejudice*), and *L'Abbaye de Northanger*, they were reprinted through the 1820s. Nor were these the only early translations.

Since there was no system of recognized international copyright, such borrowings were very common, with British publishers also producing translations of European literature quite regardless of what the original writer might think, and with no intention of offering them any payment. Books were also frequently pirated in North America: *Emma* was printed by a Philadelphia firm in 1816.

We don't think that Jane Austen was aware of what was being done with her work and it's difficult to know whether she would have been offended or delighted.

Below John Wesley Jarvis, *James Fenimore Cooper*, 1822. Cooper began his writing career with a novel called *Precaution*, perhaps in direct imitation of Austen.

Persuasion'. In 1825, a lawyer in a breach of promise (broken engagement) case in Shrewsbury mentioned that, 'In one of Miss Austin's Novels [sic], *Sense and Sensibility*, the heroine [...] expressed indignation that a man of thirty – only thirty – should dare to propose to marry her'. According to reports, everyone in the courtroom laughed. A few years later, in 1829, a short story appeared in a volume called *Friendship's Offering*, which talked in detail about Captain Wentworth and the plot of *Persuasion*, though it mistook the surname of the heroine.

This all suggests that Austen's novels were already enjoying quite a significant level of popular recognition. You don't advertise a book by saying it is reminiscent of someone obscure and nor do you make a joke in a courtroom about a writer no one has heard of; in both cases, you have to be reasonably confident that some people at least know who you're talking about.

It also indicates that the several writers who borrowed from Austen in their own work during this period were probably not committing plagiarism – as they have sometimes been accused of doing – but that instead they fully expected their readers to recognize the Austen references. It was emulation, homage. *The Refugee in America*, published in 1832 by Frances Trollope, mother of the popular Victorian novelist Anthony Trollope, borrows almost all its character names from Austen. It has been suggested that James Fenimore Cooper, author of *The Last of the Mohicans*, imitated Jane in his first novel, *Precaution*, published in 1820, while a journalist identified two other imitators in an 1828 article entitled 'Novels – plagiarisms from Miss Austen' printed in the literary journal *The Atlas*.

In order to bolster the argument for plagiarism, the article claims that Austen was obscure but it simultaneously bemoans that her novels were

Brontë on Austen

The novels of Jane Austen appear to have passed Charlotte Brontë by until she was in her thirties, when the writer and critic George Henry Lewes enthused to her about them. His enthusiasm had the fairly common effect of setting her against them. Writing to Lewes in January 1848, she claimed to have found in *Pride and Prejudice*: 'An accurate daguerrotyped portrait of a common-place face; a carefully-fenced, highly cultivated garden with neat borders and delicate flowers'. It was, to her, stifling: 'no open country – no fresh air – no blue hill – no bonny beck'. She would, she says, not enjoy living with Austen's 'ladies and gentlemen in their elegant but confined houses'.

Nor was Lewes the only man to imagine that Charlotte would enjoy Austen more than she did. In 1850 her publisher George Smith sent her a parcel of books on loan that included *Pride and Prejudice, Sense and Sensibility* and *Emma*. She did read *Emma* and liked it even less than *Pride and Prejudice*. In a letter to Smith from April 1850 she describes feeling for it 'just the degree of admiration which Miss Austen herself would have thought sensible and suitable – anything energetic, poignant, heart-felt, is utterly out of place in commending such works'.

Brontë praises the 'Chinese fidelity' and 'miniature delicacy' in the novel, but taken as a whole her response is both negative and vicious. She imagines Austen wearing 'a well-bred sneer', as being scornful and standoffish. She talks about Austen's 'business' rather than her art, and accuses her of being a superficial writer, concentrating on 'the surface of the lives of genteel English people', on actions rather than feelings. She dismissively sums her up as 'a complete and most sensible lady, but a very incomplete and rather insensible (not senseless) woman'.

Though Brontë might have responded more positively if she'd come to Austen in her own time, it is obvious that Austen's work aroused strong feelings in her, and that Austen might in some ways have been a model, if only to oppose herself to.

Opposite George Richmond, *Charlotte Brontë*, 1850. Brontë clearly resented being encouraged to read Austen's novels by male acquaintances.

'established as circulating library favourites'. It also suggests that Austen had by this point managed to acquire two different types of reader: 'the more judicious critics' who were able to appreciate her properly, and those who read her 'with an ungrateful pleasure' for simple entertainment. This is an example of the division which opened up between Austen's fans and her more self-consciously intellectual admirers.

It appears that Bentley probably didn't single-handedly save Austen. She already had quite a large audience. What he did was to help maintain her status as an author. His 'Standard Novels' volumes were all the same size, designed to be displayed at home, kept and re-read. Austen appeared alongside other famous names in Victorian homes.

Her work was frequently advertised and promoted in the 1830s and 1840s and continued to be well regarded. She was included in the *Memoirs of the Literary Ladies of England*, written by Anne Elwood, and described in a review of it in *Bell's Weekly Messenger* as 'the highly celebrated Miss Austen'. She was also admired by many male writers: the politician and historian Lord Macaulay, the poet Alfred, Lord Tennyson and the critic George Henry Lewes, who recommended her (unsuccessfully) to Charlotte Brontë. Most authors would be more than happy to receive this kind of attention and praise for newly published novels, let alone ones that were by then twenty or twenty-five years old.

Though Cassandra had been happy to publish two of her sister's manuscripts and, later, to sell off the copyrights, she was more protective of the rest of her sister's writing. It's obvious that Jane's correspondence was culled, in places heavily; there are, for example, no surviving letters for 1797, and only one written between September 1801 and January 1805. Cassandra is probably

Opposite The memorial window to Jane Austen in Winchester Cathedral, unveiled in 1901.

the person chiefly responsible and as Jane's executor and chief beneficiary, she would have been within her rights, however much we resent it. But we know that Jane also wrote regularly to Frank and Charles, and few of those letters were preserved either. Cassandra passed on what she had selected to keep to favoured relations, together with Jane's manuscripts, scattering her sister's archive among at least seven individuals.

The younger generation of Austens were proud of Jane but not reverential. At some point around the middle of the nineteenth century, Jane's niece Anna Lefroy, who published several books for children, ventured on a partial continuation of *Sanditon*, though she didn't ever finish it. In 1850, another niece, Catherine Hubback, published her first novel, *The Younger Sister.* The first few chapters are *very* closely modelled on the surviving manuscript fragment *The Watsons*, something Catherine neglected to mention, though she included a dedication to her aunt and started styling herself as a 'niece of Jane Austen' in later books. There are differences between the beginning of the published novel and the manuscript, but nearly all the names and incidents remain the same. Possibly Catherine was working from memory, but some descriptions and dialogue seem to have been lifted directly, either word for word or very nearly so. It's not impossible that her source might perhaps have been another copy of the manuscript or, conceivably, even a later draft.

It may have been in part this plagiarism, and the deaths over the next fifteen years or so of the last of Jane's siblings, that persuaded a few of her nephews and nieces to start gathering material. In December 1869 James Edward Austen-Leigh published *A Memoir of Jane Austen* with Bentley and in 1871 an expanded second edition was released, containing a summary of and extracts from *Sanditon*, and all of *Lady Susan* and *The Watsons*. Some of the profits went towards installing a new, more informative, memorial plaque above Jane's grave in Winchester Cathedral. A great-niece penned several magazine articles about her famous relation.

Though some of Jane's relatives still clung to the idea that her letters should be kept private – at least one, Frances Sophia, a daughter of Frank Austen, took it on herself to destroy a number which she had access to – the dam was broken. In 1884, Jane's great-nephew Lord Brabourne edited and published a substantial amount of her surviving correspondence, which had come into his possession after the death of his mother, Fanny Knight. Five and a half years later, in 1891, he sold ten of the letters and when he himself died in 1893, sixty-four others were auctioned off.

The *Memoir* and the letters together helped to cement Austen's popularity and her reputation even more firmly. By the end of the nineteenth century, most other writers from the Georgian period had fallen out of favour. Austen had not. She was regularly referred to as a genius, one of the best English novelists. She was included in an essay series on 'great' writers, and mentioned alongside Dickens, George Eliot and Charlotte Brontë. The novels were by now out of copyright in Britain, but publishers invested in multiple illustrations for new editions released through the 1890s, which sold extremely well. Indeed, Austen was praised and embraced and repackaged so thoroughly through the middle and later decades of the nineteenth century that you can see how she might have begun to be regarded as an honorary Victorian. There was almost no protest when, in 1900, she was included in a book entitled *Victorian Novelists*, though she had died twenty years before Victoria came to the throne.

Mementote in Dño
Joannæ Austen, obiit
mens . Iul : xviii .
A.S.D. mdcccxvii .
in judicio

Below Two of the dozens of illustrations produced by Hugh Thomson for what is sometimes called the 'Peacock' edition of *Pride and Prejudice* (1894). Publishers realised that Austen's fans were a potentially profitable market.

'Every time I read Pride and Prejudice *I want to dig her up and beat her over the skull with her own shin-bone'*

Mark Twain, letter written September 1898

Naturally, there were other dissenters besides Charlotte Brontë. Mark Twain was famously violent in his criticism of Austen, though he also admitted to re-reading her work, suggesting, surely, that even if he didn't like her, he found her compelling. But she looked to be firmly established both critically and commercially. More family memoirs found publishers, as did books by other writers, including the American biographers Oscar Fay Adams and Constance Hill.

'Austenesque' fiction – prequels and sequels, and 'variations' borrowing characters from Austen's published works – is nowadays a thriving subgenre all of its own; the first to venture on it was Sybil G. Brinton, in 1913, with a novel called *Old Friends and New Fancies*. At around the same time, Katherine Metcalfe, an English tutor at Oxford, returned to the first edition of *Pride and Prejudice* in order to create an authoritative scholarly version of the text. In 1915, the first twelve manuscript pages of *The Watsons* were one of the big-ticket items at an auction to raise money for the Red Cross while the centenary of Austen's death, in 1917, received a very respectable amount of attention, given that Britain was then at war. A plaque was put up in Chawton and another in Southampton, and plenty of articles appeared in the newspapers.

Austen is thought of nowadays as appealing more to female readers than male ones and so it is strange to find her spoken of in *The Westminster Gazette*, just before the First World War, as being 'peculiarly a man's author'. It is stranger still to find that her novels were frequently suggested as being particularly attractive and beneficial to soldiers in the trenches: 'men "out there" are devouring Jane Austen and the classic poets,' announced an article in *The Tatler* in 1918. One of the reasons given was that, supposedly, Jane's fiction refused to ever acknowledge the conflict that had raged for half her life; that it represented a tranquil, idyllic, nostalgic vision of England. In 1924, the author Rudyard Kipling published a short story called *The Janeites*, which played on this same idea.

The separation between 'mere' fans and 'true' admirers of Austen had been around for a century or so by this point, but it was becoming more exaggerated. On the one hand, Austen manuscripts and memorabilia started changing hands for startling sums – in 1930 a letter mentioning *Pride and Prejudice* was sold for £1,000. On the other hand, various academics started putting forth their interpretations of Austen and staking their claims on her. Prominent among them was Robert William Chapman, under whose name the Oxford University editions of her novels (and later on, letters, fragments and juvenilia) appeared, though he had married the Austen scholar Katherine Metcalfe and the work appears to have been largely collaborative. The editions included contemporary fashion plates, maps and even the entire text of the play that is so nearly performed in *Mansfield Park*: an admirable effort, but one which helped to fix ideas about not just the world that Austen lived in but also about which aspects of her work were important, and which were not.

And between these two extremes, the quasi-religious and the scholarly, was a public that had by no means lost its taste for Austen. Commercial publishers usually have a good idea of their market and the interwar period saw the publication of several different editions of Austen's texts, including her extravagantly silly teenage story *Love and Freindship* [sic] and a number of popular biographical and critical works. A reworking of *Sanditon* called *Somehow Lengthened* appeared, as did two continuations of *The Watsons*, one by a great-great-

Opposite Greer Garson and Laurence Olivier as Elizabeth Bennet and Mr Darcy in the 1940 film adaptation of *Pride and Prejudice.*

niece of Jane's who went on to produce *Margaret Dashwood, or Interference* and *Susan Price, or Resolution* – novels focusing on minor characters from *Sense and Sensibility* and *Mansfield Park* respectively.

T.H. White, who would later go on to write a popular Arthurian fantasy series adapted by Walt Disney, produced a detective novel in 1932 called *Darkness at Pemberley.* It has very little connection to *Pride and Prejudice* but the name was clearly considered helpful, publicity-wise. As the then-new medium of radio surged in popularity, many of Austen's novels were read or performed. In 1936 a radio version of *Love and Freindship* [sic] was broadcast. All the indications are that audiences were, or were believed to be, hungry for Austen-related content, almost regardless of its quality.

Scenes from Austen's stories had been reworked for amateur dramatic performances since the beginning of the twentieth century, though as time went by, a hierarchy of popularity began to appear, with *Mansfield Park* at the bottom and *Pride and Prejudice* at the top. This appears to have become by far the best known, with adaptations appearing under titles such as *Elizabeth Refuses* and *I Have Five Daughters.* In the 1930s the novel underwent its first (though not last) cultural 'moment', with a number of competing stage versions appearing nearly simultaneously in Britain and the United States – one scripted by A.A. Milne, author of *Winnie-the-Pooh.* Austen-inspired gowns even became briefly fashionable. Hollywood expressed an interest in the story, though delays and recasting meant that the very first screen adaptation of *Pride and Prejudice* appeared on BBC television in May 1938.

By the time the Hollywood film version arrived in British cinemas towards the end of 1940, the country was at war. Most of Europe had fallen and London had been bombed nearly every night for two months. Metro-Goldwyn-Mayer's *Pride and Prejudice* shifted the story forward in time to what, judging from the costuming, looks to be the 1830s – a decision which removed it entirely from any wartime context. It had often been claimed that Austen excluded war from her fiction, but the film solidified the idea even further.

Austen's novels were in the process of becoming fixed as fantasy: both the author and her creations removed to a dreamlike, theme-park past, with the unpleasant bits carefully stripped out. This was the version of her that was embraced and promoted. In 1940 the literary critic and psychology lecturer Denys Harding published a collection entitled *Regulated Hatred and Other Essays on Jane Austen.* He developed an argument he had made in a talk given the year before, identifying moments of darkness and of serious social criticism in Austen's work, but he was very much at odds with the prevailing popular mood.

Though the BBC's television drama unit had shut up shop for the duration of the war, radio and theatre productions of three Austen novels did continue. A seven-part radio serial of *Sense and Sensibility* was broadcast in 1944 and the several stage versions of *Pride and Prejudice* were repeatedly revived. A new theatrical adaptation of *Emma* was put on in 1943 and another the following year: both toured. Popular as those productions were, however, there seems to have been little enthusiasm during the war for adaptations of Austen's remaining novels. A play based on *Persuasion* was shown in Bath in 1940, but neither *Mansfield Park,* with its uninspiring romance between cousins, nor *Northanger Abbey* seems even to have made it onto the radio. Perhaps the fact that *Persuasion* opens in 1814, and that its hero is a naval officer just returned from years

Robert William Chapman

Robert William Chapman studied classics – Greek and Latin – in both his native Scotland and at Oriel College Oxford, before going to work for the Clarendon Press, the forerunner of the Oxford University Press. He also found time to serve in the First World War, to write for *The Times Literary Supplement* and to produce what were, for a long time, considered to be the definitive editions of Jane Austen. Critics have pointed out that the last of these achievements was greatly assisted by his wife, Katherine Metcalfe. Metcalfe had not only produced the first scholarly edition of *Pride and Prejudice* but also published, under her maiden name, her own *Northanger Abbey* with introduction and appendix in September 1923, three months before her husband's complete version of the six novels appeared with the same press. Why they should have decided not to collaborate openly remains a mystery.

By most accounts formidable and perhaps rather eccentric, Chapman was once described as the 'High Priest of Jane worship'. He elected himself Jane Austen's defender not just from textual error, but against all comers. When an Oxford professor named Heathcote William Garrod ventured on an essay entitled *Jane Austen: A Depreciation* in 1928, Chapman leapt in to disagree. He was possessive of Austen; in addition to duplicating his wife's academic work, he was quick to criticize an edition of *Love and Freindship* that he had not been involved in, and could for many years be found pronouncing on every item of Austen news with an air of calm authority.

Left Robert William Chapman elected himself Jane Austen's defender and both his editions of her novels and his opinions proved extremely influential.

of perilous combat, made it feel too real, too close to the bone. Real history edges its way into *Mansfield Park* as well, of course, as do frequent references to the navy, while *Northanger Abbey* presents both the retired General Tilney and his son, a captain in the army, as everyday villains. All three stories may have been judged inappropriate, potentially damaging to morale.

Above The booksellers and printers of Paternoster Row were bombed out in 1940, sending many older novels temporarily out of print. Second-hand copies of Austen's works were much sought-after.

Relatively few books were printed in Britain during the war, not simply because there was a shortage of paper, but because Paternoster Row, home to many London publishers and booksellers, was destroyed in the Blitz in 1940, together with stock and – what was worse – printer's plates. Many older novels went out of print for a time and a thriving second-hand trade emerged. You can find advertisements in the newspapers looking for copies of specific novels; Jane Austen often features. She had become a writer that people reached for in times of trouble.

Rudyard Kipling and *The Janeites*

Rudyard Kipling was part of the cultural elite, numbering among his relations famous painters, authors and politicians such as Edward Burne-Jones and the Conservative prime minister Stanley Baldwin. There is an undeniable and distasteful undercurrent of both intellectual and class snobbery in *The Janeites*. The story is chiefly narrated by a man called Humberstall, a London hairdresser, and it is written in an obtrusive attempt at cockney dialect that's very difficult to read. It tells how, in the trenches of the First World War, Humberstall overheard a discussion about Jane Austen and mistakenly assumed he had stumbled on a secret society. Paying for entry, he was given a few names and phrases, which did in fact turn out to be the key to obtaining protection and help from people who were otherwise strangers to him. Jane Austen saves his life. After the war he reads and re-reads the novels, evangelizing about her to all and sundry and declaring that 'there's no one to touch Jane when you're in a tight place'. Kipling also tells us, though, that Humberstall was badly injured during the war and is subject to fits, leaving us uncertain whether his obsession with Austen is the result of brain damage or of the author's powerful universal appeal. Nevertheless, the story was very popular and the term 'Janeite' still remains in largely jocular use today to describe keen fans of Austen.

"'[...]there's no one to touch Jane when you're in a tight place'"

The Janeites, Rudyard Kipling

Right John Collier, *Rudyard Kipling*, 1891. Kipling's attitude to Austen was affectionate but at the same time faintly patronising. He also wrote a poem about her, entitled 'Jane's Marriage'.

"'[...] you and I must establish a [...] club [...]'"

Emma

Given Austen's consistently high reputation through the nineteenth and early twentieth centuries, and the fervour with which a portion of her readers always responded to her, it's surprising how long it took for any organized fan club to emerge. The Brontë Society was founded in 1893, the Dickens Fellowship in 1902. Austen's admirers were not so quick off the mark.

The idea of a Jane Austen Society had been floated before the First World War by Percy Fitzgerald, who suggested in *The Sphere* the formation of 'a circle of [...] really sincere devotees, who have re-read and studied Jane Austen' and might meet at monthly dinners to discuss the books. Fitzgerald was himself an author, including of a book called *Jane Austen: A Criticism and Appreciation*. He was also a sculptor who donated two bronzes of his own creation to the Pump Room in Bath. One depicted Charles Dickens, the other Jane Austen. Dickens had in his will expressed his wish that no monuments be raised to him, but it was the bronze of Austen that caused ructions when it was installed in 1912. Indeed, after protests from Austen relations, it was removed. Though the bronze was not aesthetically appealing – it was described in an article written by Joan Austen-Leigh in 1989 as having 'an enormous nose and a vulgar leer' – this was actually quite an achievement. It also indicates that there was a certain amount of friction between the fans and the family.

This continued as the twentieth century wore on. Chawton remained in the ownership of the Knights – the descendants of Jane's brother Edward. Visitors did find their way to the cottage where Austen had lived for the last eight years of her life, but aside from the wooden plaque which had been put up in 1917 there wasn't much for them to see. The building had been split into several separate dwellings and by the 1920s also contained the village club. One reporter for *The Times* who visited in 1925 lamented its dilapidated state: the windowsills rotting, the garden overgrown, the fence falling down. The only relic of Austen's time was apparently a fireplace that was shortly to be removed to make way for a more modern grate. Though 1925 was the 150th anniversary of Austen's birth, as well as the year when the Dickens Museum in London opened its doors, lamentations were all that emerged.

It wasn't until 1940, a decade and a half after Rudyard Kipling had invented his fictional 'Society of Janeites', that the real Jane Austen Society was founded.

The Society was the brainchild of a woman called Dorothy Darnell. Born in 1876, one of many children of a vicar, Darnell had trained as an artist, studying miniature painting under the acclaimed Alfred Praga. In the late 1930s she moved to the neighbourhood of Chawton with her two older unmarried sisters. Unlike Fitzgerald, Darnell was careful to get the Austen family onside – Edward Knight, the then-owner of the Chawton estate, was one early president of the society.

The central aim was to do up Chawton Cottage and run it as a museum, and there was some initial anxiety about whether this was an appropriately patriotic use of people's time and money, given the challenges that faced Britain in the 1940s, even after the war had ended. Darnell persevered, however, and her perseverance bore fruit. The Knights agreed to sell the building's freehold, and a London solicitor named Thomas Edward Carpenter bought it for £3,000 and then donated it in memory of his son Philip, who had been killed fighting in Italy aged twenty-two, and had been, according to his father, deeply interested in Jane Austen's novels. The Carpenters would go on to give further generous donations.

Left The plaque affixed to the cottage Jane occupied in Chawton, now the Jane Austen House Museum.

Below A photograph from the early days of the Jane Austen House Museum. From left to right, Lieutenant Colonel Clement Richard Satterthwaite, who held several roles in the Jane Austen Society, Mrs Newman, an existing tenant of the cottage who acted as caretaker, Dorothy Darnell, the founder of the Jane Austen Society, and Thomas Edward Carpenter, who had bought and donated the freehold of the building.

Opposite A photograph of one of the interior rooms of the museum, showing some of the many Austen-related objects which have made their way there.

The museum opened in 1949. It was at first limited to just one room, with the rest of the house still being occupied by tenants, who also acted as caretakers. Initially there were only a handful of exhibits, and even some of those had less than perfect provenance. But the museum steadily grew, and so did the Jane Austen Society.

What was wonderful about the society was its ability to connect people, not just across boundaries of social class, occupation and experience, but also across borders. Members ranged from local enthusiasts to the Duke of Wellington. There were authors with racy private lives and a career soldier whose tennis-playing wife had publicly left him. There was more than one of the type of Oxbridge academic usually described as 'formidable'. They were all as enthralled by the recollections of Chawton families or the discovery of a tabletop said to have belonged to Jane as they were by a lock of her hair bought at auction at Sotheby's or a first edition. By 1958 about 15 per cent of the membership lived outside the United Kingdom.

It wouldn't be incorrect to see both the society and the museum as emerging not in spite of the war, but because of it. It wasn't just the Carpenter family who had lost a loved one. Dorothy Darnell had a nephew who died in France. The Duke of Wellington's nephew had been killed, too, in 1943; indeed, that was how he had come to inherit the title. It doesn't take a psychologist to see why they were so strongly drawn to Austen, who had died an untimely death in her intellectual prime, just as she began to taste success. Nor is it so strange that they shared an unreasoning yet urgent need to restore a neglected building and plant up a garden, to locate lost relics, to try to find some way back into the past.

'[...] oblivion of the past – how natural, how certain too!'

Persuasion

The times were changing, however. While some very valuable Austen artefacts were donated to the new museum, others were spirited away to America. In 1952 plans were proposed for a new bypass road that would go through Chawton, and when it was built, on a slightly different route, it effectively cut the village off. Several of the most active members of the society were growing older or were in poor health and a number passed away in the early 1950s, including Dorothy Darnell. Robert William Chapman died in 1960.

Their influence didn't vanish overnight. Mary Lascelles, a prominent Oxford academic and another Jane Austen Society member, revised Chapman's scholarly editions in the 1960s and they remained widely used in universities. That is, by the by, Lascelles as in the notorious slave-owning family, which included the Earls of Harewood and is in fact briefly mentioned by name in *Mansfield Park* – a novel for which Mary Lascelles had written the introductory essay. One wonders how many of her students felt too embarrassed or intimidated to bring the subject up in their tutorials; undoubtedly, it is difficult to challenge your own tutors, or to question ideas and interpretations which have been presented as authoritative.

The generational shift, did however, enable other academics to offer their own ideas about Austen rather more freely. But with the scholarly fashion being increasingly for broad-brush, politicized readings, those ideas were sometimes dismissive and on occasion actively critical. For Marxists, Austen's novels were too slight, too narrow; in short, limited and bourgeois. In the eagerness to develop their arguments, critics were occasionally guilty of misrepresentation. Any reader who pays reasonably close attention to Austen's fiction ought to object to assertions that her scenes are invariably set indoors or that she never writes about poor or working-class characters: these things simply aren't true.

Marxists were not the only ones to find that Austen's work resisted theorizing. In the 1970s, several more appreciative and detailed scholarly books on Austen appeared, showing that her work did in fact engage with the issues of her day. The authors arguably tipped too far away from Marxism, though, insisting – sometimes, again, in the face of the evidence – that her politics were uniformly conservative. Feminist critics struggled to fully embrace an author whose finished novels all end with their heroines getting married.

And so far as popular culture was concerned, most of the academics might as well have spared themselves the effort. *Pride and Prejudice* was adapted for British television twice in the 1950s. *Persuasion* and *Emma* both made their way to the small screen in 1960, with other Austen series appearing at intervals in the years that followed. Viewers in the United States, Australia, Spain, Italy and the Netherlands were also treated to television adaptations. There were stage plays, radio performances, even a musical and, always, a steady flow of popular books, newspaper stories and magazine articles.
The level of interest in Jane Austen remained high throughout the 1960s and 1970s, peaking in 1967 –

Opposite One of several commemorative stamps issued by the Royal Mail to celebrate the 200th anniversary of Jane Austen's birth.

Right A memorial tablet to Austen unveiled in 1967, the 150th anniversary of her death, in Poets' Corner in Westminster Abbey.

the 150th anniversary of her death – and 1975, the 200th anniversary of her birth.

In 1967 there were newspaper and magazine articles, joke obituaries, yet another version of *Pride and Prejudice* and various television specials celebrating the author. At Chawton five days of events were scheduled, starting with a speech by Edward Heath, then leader of the opposition and later prime minister, and continuing with a music recital, a film about Chawton, dramatic extracts from the novels, a cricket match in period costume, tree planting, a bonfire, and a wreath-laying ceremony at Winchester Cathedral. December of the same year saw the dedication of a memorial tablet in Poets' Corner in Westminster Abbey, placing Austen alongside other literary greats.

The celebrations in 1975 were even more of a national event. There were exhibitions not just at the museum in Chawton, but in Winchester, Scotland and at the British Museum in London. There was a concert with the programme drawn from music books linked to Austen. Bath held a week-long festival, offering lectures, walking tours around the city, dancing in the Pump Room, a chance to bathe in the Roman Baths and a performance of *Pride and Prejudice*. The Cheltenham Festival of Literature hosted a special tribute. The Post Office produced a set of commemorative postage stamps. *Sanditon* was serialized in *Woman's Own* magazine. In the week of Austen's 200th birthday, the television schedules were filled with tribute programmes.

The anniversaries attracted public attention but they also highlighted just how far into the past Austen and her novels were receding all of a sudden. Most of the founder members of the Jane Austen Society had not only been born in the nineteenth century, but would have been able to remember it as well. They are quite likely to have had grandparents whose lives had overlapped with Austen's. But by the 1970s there were fewer and fewer people who were able to say the same.

It is probably related, I think, that you can see in the second half of the twentieth century a shift towards accepting that, even if they weren't studying Austen, people were going to need more help understanding her – explanations, relics, visual cues. It's clear in the anniversary celebrations: the displays of manuscripts and artefacts, the dressing up in period costume, the pilgrimages to places that Austen had been to and written about. It's clear from the continued popularity of the television adaptations and from the value that was increasingly placed on objects, even those with only vague or indirect links to Jane Austen herself.

In 1976, the year following the 200th anniversary of her birth, the minutes of the Jane Austen Society listed a number of new accessions to the museum, including a baby's cap, a bell presented to Charles Austen, which

Georgette Heyer and the birth of Regency romance

Georgette Heyer published her first novel in 1921, when she was still a teenager, and by the time she died, in 1974, she had produced over forty books. Though there were among that number both detective stories and historical novels, the majority were Regency romances, a subgenre that, if she didn't invent it, Heyer did much to popularize. Her sales were phenomenal and she understood what audiences were looking for. Heyer's work displays almost all of the tendencies apparent in her many successors and imitators. Her heroes are usually rich or titled, and often both; her heroines are pretty and spirited but poor, or what passes for poor. There are elopements and smugglers, abductions and convoluted misunderstandings, while duplicitous villains rub shoulders with embarrassing relations and comic dogs. The stories often centre around the London social season, with Bath also being a favourite backdrop as love blooms in unlikely and yet predictable places.

What puts Heyer out of the ordinary is her historical research, which was very thorough. I have even seen it claimed that her 1937 novel *An Infamous Army*, set around the Battle of Waterloo, used to be on the syllabus at the Royal Military Academy at Sandhurst.

Contemporary reviewers often spoke of Heyer in relation to Austen; even when they were contrasting the two writers, Austen remained the closest point of comparison. Heyer's dialogue can be both funny and witty; she can marshal large casts with an impressive lightness of touch and her heroines, like Austen's, are often subject to familial pressure and manipulation. There are by now generations of readers of Austen who have read Heyer too. Several 'sequels' and continuations of Austen's novels also reveal Heyer's influence. It probably wouldn't be incorrect to see Regency romance in general as in part a commentary on Austen, an ongoing, ever-developing response to her and her fiction, but the relationship is not all one way. Our reading of Austen's novels has also been affected.

had been looted in the early 1850s from Rangoon (now Yangon, in modern-day Myanmar), and a sampler worked by a 'Jane Austen' who quite possibly had nothing at all to do with the author.

The popular Regency romance writer Georgette Heyer had realized, seemingly long before other people did, that many twentieth-century readers had only a vague, impressionistic sense of the Regency period – they didn't know what people had eaten, or how they'd dressed, what they'd read, what games they'd played or how they'd got from A to B. Her novels were always lavish with the detail: clothing, food, furniture, horses, long discussions about bonnets and snuff. In 1970 the biographer Marghanita Laski criticized her for this tendency in *The Times*, pointing out that these were exactly the kind of things that Austen had almost never felt the need to include in her own fiction. However, that didn't mean that there wasn't by this point a need for them. In fact, Laski had in 1969 published a lavishly illustrated book, not dissimilar to this one, called *Jane Austen and Her World*. Even the donnish, aristocratic Lord David Cecil was in 1978 persuaded to venture on *A Portrait of Jane Austen*, which offered biographical and historical context. Books like *In the Steps of Jane Austen* and *Jane Austen's England* followed in 1979 and 1986 respectively.

This urge to try to root Austen in history, in her family, in places and in things was belated and it didn't fully succeed. There were a number of enthusiasts who felt that ownership of the author and her legacy belonged not just to Chawton or in England, but to readers everywhere. In 1979 some of them founded the Jane Austen Society of North America, the first of many Jane Austen fan groups which have sprung up around the world. However, there were quite basic,

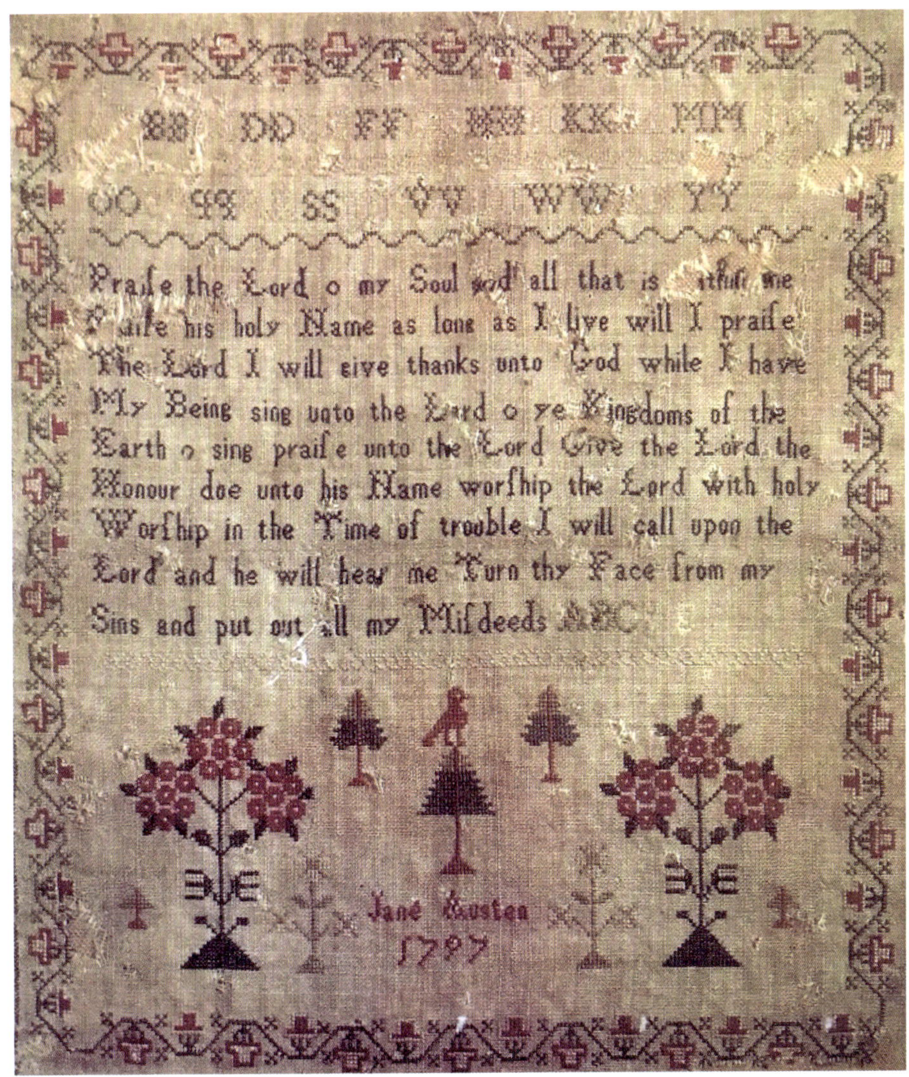

fundamental facts about the Austens which remained unknown to the public. The existence of Jane's brother George, for example, was still being ignored by many commentators into the 1980s. And the idea that Austen's work had nothing to do with the events or issues of her own time somehow managed to persist, no matter how much evidence to the contrary people presented.

Above The eagerness to collect objects related to Austen resulted in one or two slightly questionable accessions to the museum, including this sampler, which may well have been worked by a completely different Jane Austen.

Sir Charles Grandison
or
The happy Man.
a Comedy in

Dramatis Persona.
Men Women
Sir Charles Grandison Harriet Byron
Sir Hargrave Pollexfen Miss Jervois
Lord L. Milliner Lady L.
Lord G. Miss Grandison
Mr. Reeves Sally
Mr. Selby Mrs. Reeves
Mrs. Auberry
Miss Auberry
Miss Sally

The 1980s opened with a new six-part television series of *Sense and Sensibility* and, in 1983, the first British screen adaptation of *Mansfield Park*, though this proved underwhelming to reviewers. There was also a film set in the modern day, *Jane Austen in Manhattan*, about rival groups trying to stage an adaptation of *Sir Charles Grandison*, a play manuscript which may have been written at least partly by Jane and does appear to have been copied out in her handwriting. *Jane Austen in Manhattan* came from the acclaimed Merchant Ivory duo and was, unusually for them, quite poorly received. But it could be seen as part of a wider trend, its aim not to shock or surprise but to try to analyse what Austen had come to mean, to explore the different ways in which she might be reimagined, consumed and understood by a new generation.

In 1982, Jane Gardam's short story *The Sidmouth Letters* was adapted for television. It combined delicate suggestions about Jane's possible doomed seaside romance with a deep cynicism about American academia; a cynicism also visible in the figure of Morris Zapp, the Austen expert who crashes noisily through David Lodge's trilogy of campus novels, published between 1975 and 1988. In 1984 Fay Weldon's *Letters to Alice* appeared: a book of advice addressed to a modern young woman, championing the power of literature and subtitled *On First Reading Jane Austen*. Hot on its heels came a novel called *Jane Austen in Australia* or *Antipodes Jane*, which imagined that Aunt Leigh Perrot's trial for stealing lace had resulted in conviction rather than acquittal, and that she had subsequently been transported, her niece electing to accompany her. The 1987 television adaptation of *Northanger Abbey*, meanwhile, was wildly odd and highly sexualized – not perhaps all that out of keeping with the novel itself, but certainly very different from any of the screen versions of Austen novels that had preceded it.

The commodification and commercialization of Austen continued, too: 1981 saw the publication of *Dirty Bits*, a book which claimed to have compiled 'the naughtiest passages from Jane Austen, Charles Dickens, the Works of William Shakespeare and the self-styled Good Book'. It's funny, of course; you'd have to be desperate to go fumbling through *Sense and Sensibility*

Opposite, left A manuscript page of a short play adaptation of Samuel Richardson's novel *Sir Charles Grandison*, generally considered to be in Austen's writing. It may have been a collaboration with other family members.

Opposite, right Anne Baxter and Robert Powell in the 1980 film *Jane Austen in Manhattan*.

to find a naughty passage but it was not the only attempt to sex Austen up. The Rutland Arms Hotel in Bakewell, in Derbyshire, advertised a 'superb Jane Austen Honeymoon Suite'. There was a popular dating service named the Jane Austen Bureau. In the same year two music books that probably contained some pieces written out by Jane were put up for auction. The following year one of the volumes containing her teenaged stories and the manuscript of *The Watsons* fetched £231,000 – nearly five times the then-price of the average house in the United Kingdom.

In 1989 Deirdre Le Faye published *Jane Austen: A Family Record*, a book that provided a factual framework for discussions of Austen's life and was the fruit of decades of dedicated research. This appeared too late to inform the two biographies of Austen which appeared in 1984 and 1987, billed as the first serious efforts for nearly half a century. Both authors were academics but their books seem to have been intended for a wider audience. While John Halperin's research came in for criticism, Park Honan ventured on bold conjectures not altogether supported by the evidence he had been careful to collect. In this they were perhaps merely a little ahead of their time. Though Austen was by now quite a favourite in academic circles, with articles and books exploring her from all kinds of different angles, and though extensive, reliable information about her and her family was now widely available, she was about to become stratospherically popular and, in the process, leave scholarly caution far behind her.

Deirdre Le Faye

Deirdre Smith was born in 1933 in Bournemouth, on the south coast of England, though her parents had married in India and her mother seems to have hailed from a Montenegrin family with long-standing connections to Egypt.

She went to school in Reading but left at fifteen to pursue secretarial training. 'Le Faye' was a fancy of her mother's, supposedly a variant of a family surname. She eventually took an administrative job at the British Museum, spending her holidays on archaeological digs and her evenings and weekends exploring local history. She identified the graves of Jane Austen's aunt Philadelphia, cousin Eliza, and Eliza's son Hastings in a cemetery in Hampstead, and subsequently became deeply interested in the Austen family.

Befriending several surviving relatives, she was not only given access to papers, but also trusted to take them away and photocopy them, and to extend and update an earlier family record. She became the acknowledged world expert on Jane Austen, eventually publishing over a dozen books, and her work is widely considered invaluable. She was, however, only mildly fond of the novels themselves, and famously impatient of academic theorizing about them.

Below The late Deirdre Le Faye, widely considered the authority on everything to do with the Austen family.

Austenmania

"We really seem quite the fashion."

Emma

In the 1930s, a number of unrelated adaptations of *Pride and Prejudice* emerged almost at the same time. In the mid-1990s something similar happened, not with one Austen novel, but with four: 1995 saw screen productions of *Pride and Prejudice*, starring Colin Firth and Jennifer Ehle, as well as *Persuasion* and *Clueless*, a contemporary adaptation of *Emma*. A film of *Sense and Sensibility* was released in the United States at the end of 1995 and early in 1996 in Britain, and two more versions of *Emma* followed in the same year, one starring Gwyneth Paltrow, the other Kate Beckinsale. All in all, six major productions appeared over the course of just eighteen months. Some were intended for British television, others for international cinema release; some were careful and restrained, while others plumped for more dramatic or romantic or comical takes. There were significant differences in terms of budget, style and tone. Roger Michell's *Persuasion*, for example, was grubby, make-up-less and naturally lit, while *Clueless* was set in and around a Californian high school. To the media, though, they were all part of the same sudden and unexpected mushroom growth of Regency bonnets. Austen was, all of a sudden, a *bona fide* cultural phenomenon.

It had admittedly been a while since any of these novels had been adapted for the big or small screens: fifteen years in the case of *Pride and Prejudice*, longer in the case of *Emma* and *Persuasion*. But the growing consensus by the early 1990s seems to have been that Austen was distant from the modern world, outdated, perhaps even irrelevant.

There were two American films – *Metropolitan* in 1990 and *Ruby in Paradise* released in 1993 – that namechecked *Mansfield Park* and *Northanger Abbey*,

Opposite Jennifer Ehle as Elizabeth Bennet in the 1995 BBC Television adaptation of *Pride and Prejudice*.

Right Jennifer Ehle and Colin Firth as Lizzy and Darcy immediately captured the imagination of viewers.

Below Kate Winslet as Marianne Dashwood in the 1995 film adaptation of *Sense and Sensibility*, directed by Ang Lee and written by Emma Thompson, who also starred as Elinor Dashwood.

even showing characters reading and discussing the books, but then appeared to turn deliberately away from Austenian resemblances. In his 1993 essay collection, *Culture and Imperialism*, the globally prominent Palestinian-American scholar Edward Saïd criticized *Mansfield Park* and, by extension, all of Austen's work. Essentially, his claim was that, unable to acknowledge the crimes being committed in Britain's colonial dominions, Austen simply ignored them, refusing to see any connection. It's a claim that has been subjected to much discussion since, but this early-1990s impatience or irritation with Austen makes it even harder to identify quite why, just a couple of years later on, Austenmania should have exploded in the way that it did.

Video may however explain why, having begun, it lasted so long. A double video boxset of the BBC's *Pride and Prejudice* went on sale before the series had even finished, months earlier than was then the norm; the other adaptations soon followed. The mid-1990s was the point at which home video and DVD sales were starting to become significant, meaning that these Austen films and series quickly became familiar to a wide number of viewers in a way that earlier versions, particularly those shown on television, hadn't been. It's also, probably not coincidentally, when internet message boards were starting to take off. Dubbing became much easier and more sophisticated, enabling audiences around the world to enjoy material originally produced in other languages. The combination of these technological developments meant that a global fandom sprang up; millions of people were able to watch the adaptations repeatedly and then convene online to discuss them.

Global Austen

One result of Austenmania, sometimes overlooked, was that it helped to create a shared global Austen. Before the 1990s, she was still seen as innately, inescapably English: a source of national pride for Britain and, for some readers in Britain's former colonies, a prominent symbol of the culture that had for many years been presented to them as superior to their own.

Austen had been translated into a number of other European languages by the end of the nineteenth century, but those versions were sometimes extremely free and even when they were faithful, Austen's irony and careful use of vocabulary made her a challenging proposition for translators. She was a later arrival to Japan and Korea, where tentative interest in her in the 1920s had been interrupted by the rise of nationalism, and she was later reintroduced in the context of the American post-war occupation. In common with a number of other Western authors, Austen had at various points been banned from the Soviet Union, Iran and China. In some places only one or two of her novels had been translated. There were countries like Israel where the available Hebrew translations were old-fashioned and didn't appeal to younger generations of readers. Between the vagaries of politics, publishing and language, readers around the world might for many years have had very different experiences of Austen.

But the flood of adaptations, coinciding with the collapse of the Soviet Union, a period of greater cultural liberalism in China and the advent of the internet, began to change that. People increasingly had access to the same film and television programmes, and even before the diverse casting that has become popular in recent years, some of the actors cast were refreshingly unexpected. We don't make enough of the fact that Gwyneth Paltrow, who took the title role in the mid-1990s film version of *Emma*, is not only an American, but an American with Ashkenazi Jewish ancestry, or that the 1995 *Persuasion* cast the Belfast-born-and-raised Ciarán Hinds as the British naval officer Captain Frederick Wentworth – not the most straightforward choice when the Northern Irish peace process was just beginning. It is at this point that it really did start to feel for the first time that Austen belonged to everyone, equally.

Below Not only was *Bridget Jones's Diary* based on *Pride and Prejudice*, the film adaptation featured Colin Firth as a romantic hero named Darcy and Hugh Grant, who had starred in the Ang Lee *Sense and Sensibility*.

Opposite, left Billie Piper as Fanny Price in the 2007 television adaptation of *Mansfield Park*. Like the 1999 film version, it was not faithful to the book, but proved far less controversial.

Opposite, right Alicia Silverstone, Brittany Murphy and Stacey Dash in *Clueless* (1995), an updating of *Emma* to a Californian high school.

Conversely, nostalgia for a period of perceived politeness, elegance and decorum may also have had a part to play; the 1990s was a period of both grungy fashion and body shaming, hyper-sexualized yet mercilessly, joylessly judgemental.

In addition, several of the actors who appeared in these adaptations were in the news for other reasons, ranging from an embarrassing criminal conviction in the case of Hugh Grant to more than one real-life romance. Colin Firth and Jennifer Ehle were briefly a couple. Emma Thompson, who had just been through a very public divorce, met Greg Wise on the set of *Sense and Sensibility* and ended up marrying him. Many of those who had starring roles in Austen had appeared, or were about to appear, in some of the decade's blockbuster films like *Four Weddings and a Funeral*, *Shakespeare in Love* and *Titanic*.

None of this fully explains what happened, though. The showrunner of the BBC *Pride and Prejudice*, Andrew Davies, had already produced a successful adaptation of George Eliot's *Middlemarch* in 1994 and over the years that followed, costume dramas based on classic novels became almost an industry. Dickens, George Eliot, the Brontë sisters, even less widely known writers like Anthony Trollope and Elizabeth Gaskell, were all dusted off to see if they would work for television. None of them entered the zeitgeist the way Jane did.

New biographies appeared: two in 1997 – one by Claire Tomalin, the other by David Nokes – while Carol Shields and Jon Spence joined the fray in 2001 and 2003 respectively. As before, however, popular as Austen had become, some of her novels simply didn't seem to appeal. *Mansfield Park* was adapted in 1999 into a controversial film version. The book's low-key heroine Fanny Price is made to write some of Austen's energetic teenage work

and her uncle's probable exploitation of enslaved people in Antigua, having been made unpleasantly explicit, is, in the end, almost shrugged off. Responses to these changes were mixed and the concluding marriage between first cousins remained off-putting to some viewers, but the film is valuable, not least as a rare example of an Austen adaptation that elects to engage with academic arguments. *Northanger Abbey* was more or less ignored until as late as 2007, when it was included alongside new versions of *Mansfield Park* (starring Billie Piper) and *Persuasion* (with Sally Hawkins) in a 'Jane Austen Season' on ITV.

Meanwhile *Pride and Prejudice* was still, again, getting the lion's share of public admiration and attention, just as it had done before and during the Second World War. When Helen Fielding's comic newspaper column 'Bridget Jones's Diary' started in *The Independent* newspaper early in 1995, it had no relation to *Pride and Prejudice*, though the BBC series was mentioned. When the column was turned into a novel the following year, Austen's plot structure and a prominent character named Darcy were added to catch the wave of popularity. But the wave kept going. When in 2001 Fielding's novel became a film, Andrew Davies was involved and several actors from the BBC *Pride and Prejudice* were included in the cast, with Colin Firth more or less reprising his Darcy performance in modern dress. Hugh Grant also made an appearance, though as the twinkly-eyed lecher Daniel Cleaver, a very different role from the hesitant, passive one of Edward Ferrars, which he had taken in the 1995 *Sense and Sensibility*. In the film the two characters compete for Bridget's affections and at one point get into a physical fight; it's obviously on one level a joke about the two earlier Austen adaptations.

For fifteen years or so, from the mid-1990s until the end of the 2000s, Austen, or at least, *Pride and Prejudice*, looked unstoppable. The novel made a cameo appearance alongside Tom Hanks and Meg Ryan in *You've Got Mail* in 1998. Though there have been several Bollywood updatings of Austen stories, it was Gurinder Chadha's Bollywood-style English-language *Bride and Prejudice* that obtained an international cinema release in 2004.

Left Keira Knightley as Elizabeth Bennet and Matthew Macfadyen as Mr Darcy in the 2005 film adaption of *Pride and Prejudice*. Though not as influential as the BBC version, the film has many enthusiastic fans.

Below Anne Hathaway as Jane Austen in *Becoming Jane* (2007), which insisted on finding – or inventing – her a stirring romance of her own.

In 2005 came the publication of the first of the *Twilight* books, loosely but recognizably modelled on Austen's novel *Pride and Prejudice*, and another film adaptation of the story set in the 1790s, arguably the original timeframe, starring Keira Knightley and Matthew Macfadyen. This did well at the box office and gained plenty of enthusiastic fans, but the BBC series continued to be the more significant cultural influence. In 2008 ITV showed *Lost in Austen*, a four-part series about a modern-day Austen fan obsessed with *Pride and Prejudice* who ends up trapped in the novel where her presence disrupts the plot; at one point this imitated the iconic (though uncanonical) 'wet shirt' scene where Colin Firth, overheated from riding on a hot summer's day, plunges into the lake at Pemberley.

Two biopics were released in 2007. *Miss Austen Regrets* is rather sombre and draws chiefly on Austen's own correspondence. It was unfairly overshadowed by *Becoming Jane*, based on the somewhat fanciful biography by Jon Spence, which not only imagined a detailed love story for Jane and Tom Lefroy, borrowing liberally from *Pride and Prejudice*, but also showed Jane's brother George interacting with his family rather than living several miles away with carers. Then 2009 saw the publication of *Pride and Prejudice and Zombies*, an 'expanded edition' of the novel that interpolated a plague of the undead into the original text. Several other even sillier Jane Austen 'mash-ups' followed, based on some of the other novels, but only the first was made into a film.

If the runaway cultural success enjoyed by *Pride and Prejudice* after 1995 never quite extended to other Austen novels, it wasn't for want of trying. Between 2007 and 2009 new television adaptations of all five of them were produced – no mean feat, given how many

Indian and Pakistani Austen

Sense and Sensibility does have a passing connection to India and so in some ways it's apt that it should have been this novel that formed the basis of the hugely successful *Kandukondain Kandukondain* (*I Have Found It*). This came out in 2000 with the cast speaking Tamil, the language of southern India and Sri Lanka, and it explicitly politicized the story, having the Colonel Brandon character injured by Tamil separatist militants. There were other changes, including making several of the characters singers or involved in the Indian film industry, allowing for several in-jokes and for the song and dance routines that are so popular in Bollywood films. Meenakshi, the Marianne equivalent, was played by Aishwarya Rai, who would later take the lead role of Lalita Bakshi/Elizabeth Bennet in *Bride and Prejudice*.

This was another film that didn't avoid potentially sensitive issues. The cast brought together Indian actors with English, American and British-Indian ones, as well as at least one with dual heritage. Questions and frictions relating to the Indian diaspora are discussed more than once, while the British Wickham's sexually exploitative treatment of Lakhi/Lydia might be thought to mirror the rapaciousness of the East India Company or the British Raj.

Aisha, released in 2010, is often referred to as an adaptation of *Emma*, though it more closely resembles *Clueless* and, like that film, it is a fairly light rendition of the story, avoiding anything more controversial than extensive product placement. It was nevertheless still fairly successful.

Austen has also proved inspiring to several novelists from Indian and Pakistani backgrounds. Indian-American author Sonali Dev has written a series of romances set in the Indian community in San Francisco that play on Austen's originals: *Pride, Prejudice and Other Flavours*, *Recipe for Persuasion*, *Incense and Sensibility* and *The Emma Project*. In 2019 the Indian-Canadian Uzma Jalaluddin published *Ayesha at Last*, described as 'a modern and Muslim spin on *Pride and Prejudice*', while her 2023 novel *Much Ado About Nada* is based on *Persuasion*. Soniah Kamal's 2019 *Unmarriageable* is another updating of *Pride and Prejudice*, set in Pakistan; it's a clever, meaty book.

At one point Netflix planned to produce *The Netherfield Girls*, a teen *Pride and Prejudice* set in a high school and starring several Indian-American actors, and though this seems to have been delayed, it does, together with the other retellings, indicate that Austen's stories do resonate particularly strongly in the Indian subcontinent and among its diaspora communities.

One reason is probably that Austen's novels feature incidents and concerns that, in slightly different forms, are still part of many people's lives today: family obligations, for example, or arranged marriages. Another is that she was writing at a time when attitudes to all kinds of topics were in flux, long-standing ideas and conventions were being subjected to challenge and often her younger characters think very differently from their elders. This is obviously something that first- and second-generation immigrants can find themselves identifying with, particularly if their families are very religious or traditional. What strikes one reader as being of purely historical interest may, for another, be a helpful way of conceptualizing a real-life challenge or conundrum.

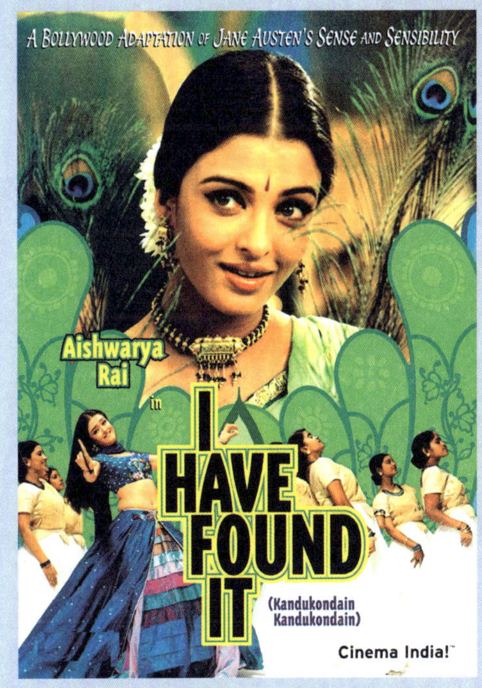

Right *Kandukondain Kandukondain* (*I Have Found It*), a Bollywood update of *Sense and Sensibility* released in 2000.

Below The 2016 film adaptation of *Pride and Prejudice and Zombies*, based on a popular rewriting which imagined the story taking place in a Britain under threat not from the French, but from a plague of the undead.

other British costume dramas set in the nineteenth century there had been (and still were) in the schedules. The first *Bridget Jones* sequel, subtitled *The Edge of Reason*, followed, vaguely, the plot of *Persuasion*. Karen Joy Fowler published a novel in 2004 called *The Jane Austen Book Club*, which was turned into a film in 2007; also set in the present day, this plays around with plots and characters from the six novels, with each one getting its chance to shine as the club progress through their reading list. Austenesque fiction multiplied exponentially through the 2000s and explored most corners of Austen's work, but the few that appeared in the reviews pages or attracted the attention of film and television production companies tended to draw on *Pride and Prejudice*. There was Jo Baker's *Longbourn*, retelling the story from the point of view of the servants, from where it appeared rather different. There was also *Death Comes to Pemberley*, a sequel in which the dastardly George Wickham is suspected of murder, written by P.D. James, a *grande dame* of British detective fiction.

This was adapted for television and was first screened on the BBC in 2013, during the overfed, soporific week after Christmas. Viewers, dozing in front of their televisions, might easily have grown confused about exactly what they were watching. Members of the cast had, between them, previously appeared in television series inspired by the works of Dickens, Thackeray, Elizabeth Gaskell, Anthony Trollope and Charlotte Brontë. One had even had a minor role in the 1995 *Pride and Prejudice*.

With a finite number of British and Irish actors available, and a tendency towards typecasting, this problem had emerged quite quickly. Lydia Bennet's best friend Mrs Forster had left Meryton only to pop up at

Right Andrew Davies, whose adaptions of classic novels have helped to shape our view not just of Austen, but of a number of other authors as well.

Mansfield Park as Maria Bertram. Jonny Lee Miller appeared alongside her as Maria's brother Edmund, and a decade later was Mr Knightley in the 2009 *Emma*, while an actor who had played a different version of Edmund Bertram took the part of the Reverend Mr Elton. The 2007 biopic *Miss Austen Regrets* brought together Olivia Williams, who had appeared in one of the two 1996 versions of *Emma*, and Greta Scacchi, who'd been in the other. They were joined by Hugh Bonneville, who had previously played the absurd Mr Rushworth in the 1999 *Mansfield Park* and was about to start shooting *Lost in Austen*. Also in the cast were Phyllida Law, who had been in the Gwyneth Paltrow *Emma* alongside her real-life daughter Sophie Thompson – aka Mary Musgrove from the 1995 *Persuasion*, the heroine Anne's self-absorbed younger sister. Sophie's own sister, Emma Thompson, had, of course, played Elinor Dashwood alongside Kate Winslet and Hugh Grant.

When the casting was deliberate, as in the first *Bridget Jones* film, it could be quite funny, but mostly it doesn't seem to have been. And the overlap also happened with screenwriters and directors – most notably Andrew Davies, who was associated not just with the 1995 *Pride and Prejudice* but with the 2007 *Northanger Abbey* and 2008 *Sense and Sensibility*, besides the *Bridget Jones* films and a whole host of other prestigious costume dramas. He would also go on to be involved with the 2019 production of *Sanditon*. The cumulative effect was to erode the differences not just between characters, but between novels and authors as well. Even new or previously unseen adaptations seemed familiar, as if they might be part of an ever-expanding and increasingly amorphous screen universe: big dresses, bonnets, carriages, Dickens, Austen, *Jane Eyre*, all swirled together.

This did Austen's less well-known work few favours. Even as the novels' individual publication bicentenaries began to be reached, from 2011 onwards, it became clear that some of them really were also-rans: they simply didn't share the same brand recognition or wide appeal.

Marvel Comics produced multi-part retellings of *Pride and Prejudice*, *Sense and Sensibility* and *Emma* in 2011 but went no further. *The Lizzie Bennet Diaries*, a web series that combined YouTube 'vlogs' (video blogs) and fictional social media profiles was greeted with popular and critical acclaim when it emerged in 2012–3; various spin-offs followed from the same creators, including *Welcome to Sanditon* and *Emma Approved*, but enthusiasm dwindled away, with one series being abandoned before it was completed. There were other Austen web series such as, for example, the *Cate Morland Chronicles* and *Northbound*, which both ran for dozens of episodes between 2015 and 2017 but these attracted much less interest – just like *Northanger Abbey*, the novel both were based on.

It was a similar story with 'The Austen Project'. Launched with great fanfare in 2013 by publisher HarperCollins, this was slated to produce modern retellings of all six of Austen's novels by well-known authors. It started two years too late to hit the publishing anniversaries and stopped in 2016 – the year before the bicentenary of Austen's death, just before the point when sales could surely have been expected to be as good as they were ever likely to be. It also only got two-thirds of the way through Austen's completed body of work. No authors were ever announced for *Mansfield Park* (Austen's Cinderella novel in more senses than one) or, more surprisingly, for *Persuasion*.

Just as *Pride and Prejudice* is the most timeless of Austen's plots, *Mansfield Park* probably is the most difficult one to move into the modern day. While you could have the Bertram family profiting from something like mining or deforestation or arms sales, there's a risk it might be seen as trivializing the horrors of Caribbean chattel slavery. And the rest of the story in some ways raises even larger difficulties. The idea of first cousins marrying each other and of children who have been raised in the same household growing up to become romantically involved are both now, for many people, uncomfortable. Yet, how do you go about creating a different-but-similar set-up, or reworking the amateur theatricals that play such an important role in the story?

In 2024, though, eight years after the Jane Austen Project folded, Nikki May did publish an updating of *Mansfield Park*, titled *This Motherless Land*, which made several large changes to the story but proved it was possible. And *Persuasion* doesn't suffer from the same issues: a few tweaks and you could easily make a twenty-first-century version work, and there have in fact been several. Clearly the difficulty of adapting the source material wasn't the only issue.

What these uncompleted projects suggest is that nearly two decades into 'Austenmania', marketing departments still didn't really understand exactly where the appeal lay. Take *Austenland*, a 2013 film based (not very closely) on a 2007 novel. Its publicists made much of the fact that the leading creatives were all women and even spoke bullishly about catering for underserved female audiences. The producer was Stephenie Meyer of *Twilight* fame, and you might think, on the evidence of her previous success, that she did know what women were looking for, but at times the film even appears contemptuous of the very audience it was presumably aimed at. It centres on a naïve Mr Darcy obsessive who travels to a 'Jane-Austen-themed' holiday park that has almost no connection to either Austen's fiction or the historical period she lived in. There's a sexual assault subplot but also some attractive, occasionally half-clothed male actors with minimal backstories. It's really quite confused, but it's indicative of wider confusion.

By the mid-2010s, with the 200th anniversary of her death fast approaching, Austen was surrounded by uncertainty and disagreement, and not just about what the market would stand. There were the fans – a huge number of them, apparently hungry for any and all Austen-related content. There were the supposedly pernickety 'Janeites', obsessing over minutiae, who could always be relied upon to provide a journalist with an outraged quote, and the academics who were able to interpret the same passage a hundred different ways.

When campaigners successfully argued for the newest English banknote design to feature a woman, Jane Austen was the one they selected. There followed vicious anti-feminist trolling and violent threats, and also endless complaints regarding the design: the quotation the Bank of England had selected, the decision to have a line drawing of Jane's rich brother Edward's house in the background, the choice of portrait. The Bank used one based on Cassandra's inexpert effort prettified to Victorian tastes – familiar, and the safest choice.

There were, however, at least two other potential candidates that attracted considerable public attention in the 2010s. One was a pencil sketch championed by the Austen biographer Paula Byrne in a BBC documentary in 2011, which shows a middle-aged woman in the act of writing. The other was the so-called Rice portrait – a large and charming painting of a pretty girl in white with short brown hair. Its provenance is fairly good, but opinion on whether this girl is Jane is divided, one major reservation being that her own immediate family seems to have been completely unaware of the picture's existence. Who could say with any confidence, though, which of these images provided us with the real Jane Austen?

When Whit Stillman directed an arthouse adaptation of Jane's early literary effort *Lady Susan* under the title *Love & Friendship* in 2016, reviewers cooed about how new and unexpected, and shockingly amoral and racy it all was. The story had first been published in the 1870s by the author's own nephew and nobody had seemed particularly shocked by it then,

Opposite, left The £10 note featuring Jane Austen, first issued in 2017, the 200th anniversary of her death.

Opposite, right J.J. Field, Bret McKenzie and Keri Russell in the 2013 film adaptation of *Austenland*, based on Shannon Hale's 2007 novel.

Opposite, below Whit Stillman's *Love & Friendship* (2016) starred Kate Beckinsale. Despite the misleading name, it was actually an adaptation of Austen's story *Lady Susan*.

but by this point there were many Austens, bearing little or no relation to one another, or, on occasion, to established biographical or historical facts. There was one Austen who was a shrinking spinster violet and another who made jokes about homosexuality in the Royal Navy. She had apparently written both fluffy chick-lit and cutting social satire. Her novels managed to engage with current affairs and political issues while simultaneously ignoring them entirely. She was a feminist and at the same time a conservative whose marriage plots were set in a peaceful sun-dappled rural England that proved uncomfortably attractive to some American far-right commentators.

Publishers released a slew of Austen-related books for 2017. Articles and documentaries were commissioned by the dozen. Plans were announced for yet another adaptation of *Pride and Prejudice* – a 'darker' and 'less bonnet-y' one. The new Austen banknote came into circulation. There were academic conferences and services of thanksgiving. But there was less agreement than there ever had been before as to exactly who, or what, was being celebrated.

Festivals and fans

The Jane Austen Centre in Bath opened its doors in 1999. It is located at 40 Gay Street, not far from No. 25, where Austen lived for the better part of a year, though that time did include visits to family. The Centre was founded in response to popular demand, and became a useful focal point for the visitors who began flooding into the city as interest in Austen grew. It had a more innovative attitude to publicity than the museum at Chawton, commissioning a waxwork of Jane, for example, and in 2014 arranging to break the record for the largest gathering of individuals in Regency dress. Being located in a city with good transport links, it was also in a position to set up an annual Jane Austen Festival.

Having run since 2001, this now extends to ten days of events each September. A typical programme features plays, talks, night-time stargazing, and workshops on dancing, fencing and Regency-era crafts. Attendees usually dress in period costume and can even get their hair done in historically appropriate styles. Trips are arranged to sites associated with Austen, and to filming locations. There are balls, breakfasts and promenades.

Those who want to dance or dress like Jane Austen and her characters aren't restricted to Bath or the festival, however. Austen fandom has grown to resemble some of the other really substantial fan groups. There are conventions and conferences, talks and tea parties and Regency balls taking place all over the world. Often these are organized by local Jane Austen societies, but not invariably. Social media connects fans with one another across huge distances. Like cosplaying or historical re-enactment, being an Austen fan can offer everything from a bit of fun to a consuming hobby, from a one-off event to a whole new community. There are even Austen influencers and podcasters who have been able to turn being a fan into a paying proposition.

Present Day

"'I wonder what will become of her!'"

Emma

The promised 'less bonnet-y' *Pride and Prejudice* never materialized but a new kind of Austen – or Austen-adjacent – content did.

In 2018, Brazilian viewers were treated to *Orgulho e Paixão* (*Pride and Passion*), 161 episodes of an Austen-inspired *telenovela* with plots and characters from different stories mixed together. The same year brought the British premieres of both a jukebox musical, *Pride and Prejudice* (*sort of)* and Laura Wade's metafictional stage continuation of Jane's novel-fragment *The Watsons*. The popularity of the improvisation troupe *Austentatious* and their fast, frenetic performances inspired by suggestions from the audience increased apace.

All of these productions seemed to channel some of the spirit of Austen's rambunctious early literary efforts. They were clever, knowing. They were prepared to be irreverent, even iconoclastic; to poke fun, to identify conventional expectations and then throw them out of the window. Even though performers were dressed in an approximation of the Regency costume made familiar by all the period adaptations, that was as far as the similarities went.

When the heroine of *The Watsons* discovers that she is trapped in a story without an ending, her reaction is to get drunk and find someone willing to relieve her of her virginity. Two other characters plan to escape and live together in sapphic bliss. *Pride and Prejudice* (*sort of)* shows Charlotte Lucas pining for Elizabeth Bennet. *Orgulho e Paixão*, relocated to early twentieth-century South America, was widely considered unsuitable for children. Often servants shouldered their way to the forefront of the action; there was feminism, music produced by instruments other than the harp and piano, regional accents and diverse casting.

Opposite One of the cast of *Austentatious*, a popular Austen-inspired improv group.

Opposite Suranne Jones in *Gentleman Jack*, which aired between 2019 and 2022. She played the eponymous 'Gentleman', the unconventional real-life heiress Anne Lister, born in 1791.

Backing away from what had become the norms of costume drama, these shows found themselves meeting historical fact. Not everyone in Jane Austen's world had been rich or well spoken or white – or, for that matter, heterosexual.

In 2015 the BBC had started showing a new series of *Poldark*, adapted from Winston Graham's popular series of historical novels, which eventually ran for five seasons. Concentrating on the earlier novels, set in Cornwall in the 1780s and 1790s, the series was shot in some beautiful locations and employed a number of very good-looking actors and actresses, but the world it revealed was a grim, grimy one and not just because the hero owns a mine. Though often venturing into melodrama, Graham's novels were the product of extensive research, which meant that war and social and economic unrest were central to his plots. Many of his characters came from poverty. Children kept dying. Though the lead actor was frequently pictured in his shirtsleeves and compared to Colin Firth, the contrast to the glossier breed of Austen adaptation was very marked.

Early in 2019 the BBC broadcast *Gentleman Jack*, a series based on the real-life story of the wildly unconventional early nineteenth-century Yorkshire heiress Anne Lister, and featuring several of her female lovers – though not the dual-heritage woman with whom she was involved as a schoolgirl.

By the time Andrew Davies's *Sanditon* appeared on television screens in the latter half of 2019, it was initially in danger of looking old-fashioned in comparison, in spite of including scenes of naked swimming and open-air sexual shenanigans as well as featuring a Black actress in the cast. The makers of the show appear to have wanted it to be modern and sexy, accurately researched but fun, popular but issue-led, all at the same time. They had consulted a number of experts. But it would in any case be difficult to attach a historically convincing middle and satisfactorily romantic ending onto an unfinished draft. With a text like *Sanditon*, and so many and such contradictory aims, it proved impossible.

All the original Austen text had been used up before the end of the first episode and the series soon ran into issues of its own devising. Charlotte Heywood was made the heroine, as the existing fragment of the story seems to indicate. Sidney Parker was made the lead male, an understandable decision reached by the majority of those who have tried their hand at finishing the story. We are told that he's good-looking. He drives a carriage, he likes a joke, and there are, anyway, no other credible candidates. But in this case Sidney was also turned into Miss Lambe's guardian, previously involved, for several years, in business in the Caribbean.

Miss Lambe is Austen's only canonically biracial character. Canonicity proving insufficient protection, however, the actress who took the role was subjected to distressing racist harassment. The storylines invented for her didn't necessarily help matters. Her character, 'Georgiana' Lambe, is repeatedly othered and belittled by some of the unpleasant people she encounters. Her Black suitor is linked to the Sons of Africa, a real abolitionist campaign group founded by men who had themselves been enslaved (though active several years earlier than the period when *Sanditon* must be set). He turns out, however, to be a habitual gambler and his boastfulness leads to her being abducted. Sidney then rescues her. In other words, a Black woman is put at risk by a Black man and saved by a White character implicated in the slavery that at this point still continued in Britain's overseas territory.

Below Mia Goth (left) and Anya Taylor-Joy in the ravishingly beautiful 2020 adaptation of *Emma*, directed by Autumn de Wilde and released just before pandemic restrictions took effect.

'Sidney Parker was about 7 or 8 & 20, very good-looking with a decided air of Ease & Fashion and a lively countenance.'

Sanditon

The makers of *Sanditon* wanted viewers to think about painful historical wrongs but they also wanted them to lust after Sidney and root for him to get together with the heroine. There were beautiful dresses and glittering ballrooms and picnics and carriages, and there were also disturbing scenes of sexual grooming and coercion, some of them incestuous. The producers came up with a self-made builder-architect defying class snobbery and an authentic-sounding Regency-era medical man, but they also added stock characters: a rich lord, a foolish vicar. Reality and several different types of fantasy were at war – the women were proto-feminist go-getters, ever ready to leap on top of an overturned carriage, but at the same time they were the passive victims of men, of illness or of their own tender hearts, waiting for someone to come and rescue them.

Sidney did declare both his rejection of slavery and his love for Charlotte but the series concluded with his decision to save his siblings from financial disaster by marrying a rich woman and getting his hands on her fortune. It turned out he wasn't an Austen hero, not even one of the less appealing ones. There was no meaningful redemption for him, and no plot resolution for either Charlotte, or Georgiana.

It was a bold way to finish and fans were outraged. Though viewing figures hadn't been particularly strong, a successful campaign was launched to persuade the production company to finish the story properly. Two further series followed, filmed back-to-back in 2021. Sidney was written out and a new love interest introduced for Charlotte and Georgiana Lambe was finally provided with some more satisfactory plotlines. Eventually, the audience did obtain its longed-for happy ending.

The 2020 film of *Emma*, starring Anya Taylor-Joy and Johnny Flynn, was an altogether simpler and more straightforward proposition than *Sanditon*. Beautifully shot, still more beautifully costumed, sweet and a touch insubstantial, it suffered from being released in February 2020, just before the pandemic lockdowns.

That same year was also when issues surrounding race and racial justice took centre stage, meaning that when Netflix's *Bridgerton* was unleashed on the world that December, it seemed to be representative of more than one major cultural shift. Here at last was a lavish television costume drama with a diverse cast; fun, frivolous roles for actors and actresses of colour; none of the typical costume drama coyness but instead frequent, though tasteful and (mostly) narratively justified, sex scenes. The source material – a best-selling series of Regency romance novels by Julia Quinn – was popular rather than prestigious 'classic' literature and American rather than British.

Inspired by the disputed theory that George III's wife, Charlotte, had Black ancestry, *Bridgerton* asked viewers to imagine an alternate history in which Britain had abolished slavery in the middle of the eighteenth century, and gentry and aristocratic circles had become ethnically diverse. Indeed, any resemblance to real events and characters appeared to be there almost by accident. There was not a glimpse of the Prince Regent (later George IV), nor of his many brothers and sisters, a dozen of whom lived to adulthood and several of whom were prominent on the London social scene. The Napoleonic Wars were briefly mentioned, but then mostly forgotten about again, lost in a whirl of balls and clothes, unlikely love affairs and unlikelier plot contrivances. Dukes and earls and baronets abounded, as they tend to in Regency romance, though even Georgette Heyer often preferred a plain 'Mr' for a hero and few of Austen's male love interests have any kind of

FROM SHONDALAND
BRIDGERTON

Opposite A promotional image for the second series of Netflix's *Bridgerton*, adapted from the novels by Julia Quinn. From left to right: Simone Ashley as Kathani Sharma, Jonathan Bailey as Anthony Bridgerton and Charithra Chandran as Edwina Sharma.

unearned title, even in her earliest work. In the background of almost every *Bridgerton* episode were dozens of nameless maids and footmen, while the middle classes and agricultural labourers alike were mostly conspicuous by their absence. There was luxury and endless consumption and no discussion of where exactly the money was coming from to finance it all.

Bridgerton was a hit, attracting huge audiences and sparking conversations about history and representation and the burgeoning popularity of romance, an already large but fast-growing publishing genre. Naturally, it attracted criticism as well. Historical costume specialists complained about the clothes, especially the allegedly poorly fitted corsets. Viewers moaned – as they had done with *Sanditon* – about the inaccurate hairstyles and headgear. There were debates about whether the cast was sufficiently diverse, and also about whether the show risked trivializing the realities of slavery and colonialism, and erasing the cruelties and racism to which millions had been subjected.

A 2023 spin-off, *Queen Charlotte: A Bridgerton Story*, did introduce the Prince Regent and his siblings, as well as his daughter Princess Charlotte, for many years second in line to the throne: her death in childbirth in 1817 was a central plot point. The main show, however, continued on its merry counter factual way, with the queen and the unwell George III the only British royals ever shown. It was fantasy and didn't pretend to be anything else. The showrunners concentrated on giving the audience what they wanted and though some of that was the familiar tropes of Regency romance, a significant part of it was Austen.

A lot of *Bridgerton* was filmed against the honey-coloured stone of Bath city centre, the setting for a number of Austen adaptations. On occasions, shots were reproduced almost frame for frame. In the second series, the male lead went for an impromptu swim and the camera lingered on his torso in a wet white shirt, a *Pride and Prejudice* in-joke that attracted media attention even though it fell far short of the nudity the show frequently featured.

Austen also served as a sort of guardian spirit, hovering over the action. Characters, inadvertently eavesdropping, hear wounding comments about themselves, as occurs in both *Pride and Prejudice* and *Persuasion*. In one series a young unmarried woman is alone in a moving carriage with a man who makes advances towards her, something which also happens to the heroine of *Emma*. Since the same young unmarried woman mentions the novel by name in another scene, the echo must be deliberate, even though in *Bridgerton* it all plays out rather differently. In what we might assume is a reference to the character of Colonel Brandon's young ward Eliza in *Sense and Sensibility*, an extramarital pregnancy hovers in the background of one season. A put-upon young woman, one of three daughters, brings to mind Anne Elliot as well as Cinderella. *Bridgerton* also aims to reproduce Austen's social commentary and witty turns of phrase, featuring an anonymous gossip sheet that exposes scandals among the upper classes and is at times turned into an ironical narrative voice.

Bridgerton was not the first period drama to experiment with diverse casting but it made it visible and it made it mainstream, very rapidly. An adaptation of *Persuasion* was announced in 2020 with a biracial actor attached as Captain Wentworth and was apparently a step too far for some. That project was mothballed, for a variety of reasons, and when another diversely cast *Persuasion* appeared two years later, criticism focused almost entirely on the decision to

Right Jane Austen-themed merchandise now extends as far as rubber ducks and tarot decks.

Below A scene from *Fire Island* (2022). Directed by Andrew Ahn, the film is a superficially raunchy but essentially romantic LGBTQ+ updating of *Pride and Prejudice*.

remake the restrained, intelligent Anne Elliot as a wine-guzzling klutz. The decision to have the Musgroves played by biracial actors and actresses elicited very little comment, and the fact that the actor who took the role of Captain Wentworth was partly Armenian none whatsoever. In 2024 the US Hallmark Channel, which specializes in commercial, made-for-television romance films, produced a *Sense and Sensibility* with a largely Black cast.

Perhaps the most noticeable change since 2017 has been the opening-up of Austen to diverse and inclusive casts and reworkings. There have been a growing number of LGBTQ+-friendly takes, including the web series *Rational Creatures*, a reworking of *Persuasion*, and multiple novels that switch the gender of Austen's heroes or heroines. *Fire Island*, brought out in 2022, relocated *Pride and Prejudice* to a gay party resort. The two leads are played by an Asian-American actor and one with dual European and Filipino ancestry. No one even blinked. There are some raunchy scenes but the film has a romantic heart. The most erotically charged moment is probably when Noah and Will (the Lizzy and Darcy equivalents) sit together on the beach, reading their respective books. The culmination shows the pair sharing a relatively chaste kiss. Though the opening has Noah quoting the first line of *Pride and Prejudice*, amused at how completely different his own priorities are, it turns out that he can't escape the plot. None of the characters is in want of a wife, but quite a few of them are looking for someone to love and build a shared future with.

You can't just put *Pride and Prejudice* back on the shelf and forget about it. It's far too big for that now. In the second half of 2024 plans for screen adaptations of no fewer than four separate versions of the story were announced: Soniah Kamal's *Unmarriageable*; Ibi Zoboi's young-adult updating, *Pride*; Janice Hadlow's *The Other Bennet Sister*, which focuses on the neglected middle Bennet child, Mary; and a new Netflix series of the original novel.

Jane Austen has come a long way from the rectory house in Steventon. There are Jane Austen societies not just across Europe and North America, but also in Japan, Singapore, Brazil, Mexico, the Middle East and Australasia. Her work has been read and re-read, loved and hated, pored over by scholars, reached for as a solace, translated into dozens of languages and transposed into formats she could never have imagined existing: radio, television, podcasts, manga. There's even an Austen AI chatbot, and one based on Elizabeth Bennet.

There are two museums dedicated to her and an annual festival in Bath. She's on a banknote. Austen's surviving letters and manuscripts, and the few pieces of jewellery that she owned, are considered very nearly priceless. Several have been saved for the nation. Even the shirt that Colin Firth wore in the 1995 *Pride and Prejudice* was bought for £25,000 by a Yorkshire museum.

You can buy Jane Austen-themed recipe books and jigsaws, tarot packs, board games, computer games, embroidery patterns, copies of the topaz cross her brother bought for her. Internet memes featuring Austen quotes (and misquotes) proliferate.

You could make an argument for several authors having influenced the way we talk and think, and Austen is one of them, but she has also helped to shape the way people feel, all over the world, and she seems still to be

Right Synnøve Karlsen as the young Cassandra and Patsy Ferran as Jane in the 2025 BBC adaptation of Gill Hornby's *Miss Austen*.

Below Pablo Pauly and Camille Rutherford in the 2024 film *Jane Austen a gâché ma vie* (*Jane Austen Wrecked My Life*), written and directed by Laura Piani.

doing it. A recent non-fiction book, *In Search of Mr Darcy*, blames her for setting apparently unrealistic romantic expectations. There's a novel called *Jane Austen Ruined My Life* and an unrelated French film, released in 2024, titled *Jane Austen a gâché ma vie – Jane Austen Wrecked My Life*. Not a positive achievement, perhaps, but, for a woman born 250 years ago, a pretty remarkable one.

Born into an era of rapid change and revolutionary ideas, forced to accept that some of her relatives and close family acquaintances – slave owners, East India Company executives – were widely considered anathema, she was compelled to become, and remain, an independent thinker. And poised as she was, uncertainly, between social classes, with a family that extended across the globe, her interest and awareness stretched far beyond the genteel drawing rooms of southern England out into the world beyond. Educated chiefly by books, primed by the example of the generation of female authors that had preceded her, the novel was her natural element and she did extraordinary things with it.

She was lucky, too. She found, eventually, a publisher who championed her, found a home on the shelves of circulating libraries and found generations of admiring readers. Perhaps even the misleading memoirs written by her family were lucky, and the destroyed letters. Even now, some of the details of her life remain mysterious. Was she ever in love? How did she really feel about some of the decisions her parents made? We can see, or think we see, echoes and suggestive similarities in her fiction: the sort that make us want to keep reading. We can uncover all kinds of things in the novels – romance, politics, cynicism, gentle humour, fierce feminism. Austen's work has been subjected to a wild and wonderful variety of readings and misreadings, and inspired millions of words of literary scholarship, but no one interpretation has ever won out, and it probably never will.

The fiction fascinates us – of course it does – but so does the woman who created it. We feel that we know her, and yet, in truth, even now, we know very little about her. Early in 2025 the BBC broadcast a series called *Miss Austen*, adapted from the novel by Gill Hornby, the first of several she has written about the Austen family. Exploring Cassandra's likely censorship of Jane's correspondence, and the relationship between the sisters, it comes up with a compelling story, but it is only one imagined possibility.

Jane Austen may have been the romantic some think she was. She may have been the incisive, far-sighted, brilliant woman that others have seen. It's not a new idea, this. A century ago, we can find a reader in the *Daily News* chiding those who imagined that Austen was 'not aware of entirely everything her world contained', her 'hawk-like intellect [...] obscured by India muslins'.

It doesn't matter that there are things we don't know about her. It doesn't even matter that we have no real idea what she looked like. She is whatever we want, or need; the glue that has brought people together, a teller of timeless stories, a guide and a comfort, a route back into thinking about the past and a mirror to the present. The worlds she created are there for us to explore and keep exploring, always the same and always changing.

End Notes

The Rectory

Jane's christening took place on 5 April 1776, nearly four months after her birth.

In common with a number of other colleges, St John's College Oxford reserved a number of places for those who could show that they were 'Founder's Kin'. The Austen boys were descended, via their mother, from a sister of Sir Thomas White, the man who had set up the college in the 1550s.

In one letter of 4 January 1820, Mrs Austen seems to suggest diverting her brother Thomas's dividend payments to her widowed daughter-in-law Mary Austen, something she had no right to do.

See Will of Cassandra Austen, Widow of Chawton, Hampshire, National Archives, PROB 11/1722/313

Jane Payne, *née* Hampson, served Princess Augusta of Saxe-Gotha, the mother of George III.

The marriage record for William Austen and Rebecca Walter, *née* Hampson can be found via genealogy websites and gives the date of the ceremony as 13 January 1727/8 – that is, what we would term January 1728. The date for the christening of their first child is given as 14 September 1728, that is, the same year, eight months after the wedding. It is entirely possible that she was premature and was baptized straight away. There does however seem to have been some mystery attached: a letter written by William Austen's aunt indicates that the couple concealed the fact of the marriage from their families for several months.

See the will of Rebecca's first husband, Will of William Walter of Gloucester, Gloucestershire, PROB 11/630/93

For evidence that Tom Lefroy loved Jane Austen with a 'boyish' love, we are forced to rely on a letter written by Tom's nephew, Thomas Edward Preston Lefroy, who married his second cousin Anna Lefroy, Jane Austen's great-niece.

Revolution

There appears to be a brief reference to French refugees in *Sense and Sensibility*. Mrs Dashwood gives both Lucy Steele and her sister 'a needle book made by some emigrant'. The word, in the absence of any additional information, most commonly denoted those who had fled the revolution.

Army and Navy

This famous quotation of Wellington's comes to us via the recollections of Philip Henry Stanhope. Stanhope became quite a well-regarded historian and his 1888 book *Notes of Conversations with the Duke of Wellington, 1831-1851* is apparently based on contemporaneous or near-contemporaneous records.

Give a girl an education

'Mrs Cawley' is listed as one of the subscribers to planned road improvements in Turl Street in the *Oxford Journal* (6 July 1782, page 2), possibly indicating that she lived on or near the road.

Will of Anne Sharp, Spinster of York Terrace Everton near Liverpool, National Archives PROB 11/2167/334.

The sixty-nine manuscript diary volumes written by Fanny Austen Knight (later Lady Knatchbull) span the years from 1804 to 1872 and are held by the Kent History and Library Centre archives, U951/F24/1-69.

The (fairly short) play adaptation of Richardson's lengthy 1753 novel *Sir Charles Grandison* is currently held by Chawton House Library. It appears to be in Jane Austen's handwriting but whether it is solely her work is another question;

family tradition suggests there was some degree of collaboration.

Jane Austen's name appeared several times in newspapers, in the *Hampshire Chronicle*, for example, (6 September 1813, page 4) and in lists of arrivals at Bath.

Written by John Fletcher in the first quarter of the seventeenth century, *The Chances* was revived by the popular actor-manager David Garrick in the 1770s. *Bon Ton, or High Life Below Stairs* is Garrick's own work, first performed in 1775, while *The Sultan, or a Peep into the Seraglio* was written by Garrick's enemy Isaac Bickerstaffe. *Tom Thumb* is presumably one of two plays of this name by the novelist Henry Fielding.

City

Mary Cassandra Twistleton was a relation of Jane Austen's (her grandmother was Mrs Austen's first cousin). Mary Cassandra eloped as a teenager but in 1798 her husband successfully sued her alleged lover, receiving £5,000 in damages, and subsequently started divorce proceedings. At this point that required the passing of a specific, personalised divorce bill. The newspapers reported all the details with salacious glee.

The description of Mrs Leigh Perrot's trial, including the presence of unnamed female supporters, appears in the *Bath Journal* (7 April 1800, page 4).

Susan is mentioned several times in Crosby & Co.'s newspaper advertisements in July and August 1803, referred to as being 'in the press', that is, at least some way into the printing process.

4 Sydney Place was a sublet, offered at a 'very low' rent with 'three years and quarter' of the lease left to run. See *Bath Chronicle and Weekly Gazette* (21 May 1801, page 1).

Countryside

Humphrey Repton, *Observations on the Theory and practise of Landscape Gardening* (1803, 1805). For the reference to turning estate inhabitants into part of the landscape design, see page 138.

Seaside

For the details about Brighton, see John Feltham, *A Guide To All The Watering And Sea-Bathing Places* (1815) pages 105–142. Feltham also mention 'Mahomed's baths', which he says are 'kept by a native of Turkey' (118). In fact they seem to have been those run by Sake Dean Mahomed, who had been born in India, and also set up one of the first Indian restaurants in Britain.

Empire and slavery

Azar Hussein, 'The Boys at Steventon: Mr. Austen's Students 1773–1796', *Persuasions Online*, Vol. 44, No. 1 (Winter 2023).

The letter from Christopher Wordsworth to Henry Handley Norris can be found in the Bodleian Special Collections, MSS. Eng. lett. b. 38, c. 789–91; Eng. misc. b. 439, c. 942, d. 1367, Folio 51–2

Legacies

Will of Jane Austen of Chawton, Hampshire, National Archives PROB 11/1596/208; Will of Cassandra Elizabeth Austen, Spinster of Chawton, Hampshire, National Archives PROB 11/2015/93

For the breach of promise case, see the *London Morning Herald* (21 March 1825, page 3), as well as numerous other newspapers.

The description of Fitzgerald's bronze comes from Joan Austen-Leigh, 'My Aunt, Jane Austen', *Persuasions* 11, 1989, pages 28–36.

The original report as to the state of 'the novelist's home at Chawton' appeared in *The Times* (1 January 1926, page 9).

Details are drawn from the minutes of the Society.

Marghanita Laski, 'The Appeal of Georgette Heyer', *The Times*, 1 October 1970, page 16.

Rudyard Kipling's 'The Janeites' first appeared in *The Storyteller*, May 1924.

Austenmania

The planned 'darker', 'less-bonnet-y' version of *Pride and Prejudice* was first mentioned in the *Radio Times* magazine (online 7 August 2017).

Present Day

The reference to Austen's 'hawk-like intellect' comes from the *Daily News* (31 March 1925, page 8).

Index

A

Index

L

Picture Credits

pp.6, 8, 11 below, 16, 20-21, 22, 24, 26, 28–29, 30, 32, 33, 35, 38-39, 44, 47, 50, 51, 52–53, 54, 56, 61 above, 67, 72, 80, 83, 86, 87, 88, 90, 91, 93, 94, 96, 98, 106, 108, 110, 112, 118, 119, 121, 123, 124–125, 133, 134, 135, 136, 138, 140 top left and below, 143, 144, 145, 146, 148, 157, 158, 160, 163, 164, 166 above, 167, 168, 172, 174, 176, 178, 179, 180, 181, 182-183, 184, 186, 188, 190, 192, 194, 196 below, 198 below courtesy of Alamy; pp.10, 59, 61 below, 71 above, 105, 111, 151 below, 154 courtesy of Bridgeman Images; pp. 11 above, 92, 166 below courtesy of Jane Austen's House, Chawton; pp.12-13 courtesy of The Paul Mellon Collection at the Virginia Museum of Fine Arts; p.19 image reproduced courtesy of Jane Austen's House. From the collection of Judy and Brian Harden; p.25 © Derby Museums/Bridgeman Images; pp. 30, 162 © National Portrait Gallery, London; p.31 Royal Collection Trust/© His Majesty King Charles III, 2025/Bridgeman Images; pp.36–37, 127 photo © Tom Graves Archive/Bridgeman Images; p.41 © photo Josse/Bridgeman Images; p.42 Fordyce, James. Sermons to Young Women. United States, M. Carey, 1809/Public domain; p.46 courtesy of the National Library of Scotland; p.49 courtesy of Brighton & Hove Museums Collections; p.58 © London Metropolitan Archives/Bridgeman Images; p.61 courtesy of British Library archive/Bridgeman Images; p.77 photo © Philip Mould Ltd, London/Bridgeman Images; p.84 photo © Victoria Art Gallery; pp.102–103 courtesy of The Morgan Library & Museum; p.131 © The British Sporting Art Trust/Bridgeman Images; p.152 courtesy of Bibliothèque nationale de France (BnF), département Littérature et art, Y2-15121; p.171 photo © Brenda Cox; p.187 © Laughing With Lizzie; p.198 above photo Robert Viglasky, © Bonnie Productions Ltd; pp.8–9, 27, 34, 62, 68, 75, 79, 82, 99, 104, 114, 128, 139 courtesy of Getty; pp.17, 55, 84, 120, 126 courtesy of Wellcome images; pp.15, 48, 63, 76, 85, 86, 90, 116–117, 132, 140 above left, 150, 153, 169 courtesy of Wikipedia.

Acknowledgements

All books are collaborative efforts, and that's especially the case with one like this. Thank you to my editors, Philip Cooper, and the endlessly patient and well-organised Charlotte Frost, and to book designer Wayne Blades, cover designer Isabel Eeles, illustrator James Oses and editorial assistant Izzy Toner, for her thorough picture research. Thank you to copyeditor Anna Watson, proofreader Daniela Nava and indexer Helen Snaith. The credit for production goes to Alex Merrett. Thank you, too, to my publicist Zoë Champion, and to Lewis Laney.

Anyone who writes about Jane Austen owes a debt to the countless editors, academics, historians and writers who have preceded them and I am certainly no exception. In particular, the Oxford World's Classics editions remain my go-to texts for Austen and the work of Deirdre Le Faye has been constantly to hand. As well as expressing my gratitude to Rhian Dolby at Hampshire Archives and Local Studies I'd also like to extend it to all those whose work in archives, picture libraries and record offices helps to make this kind of project possible.

Thank you to Sophie Andrews for providing a photograph of one of her Regency balls, and to Gill Hornby for facilitating access to stills of *Miss Austen*, the recent television adaptation of her novel of the same name. Friends and colleagues at the Oxford Centre for Life Writing at Wolfson College offered encouragement and suggestions alongside many hours of stimulating discussion about all things life-writing-related and I'm grateful for their time and insight. Thanks are also due, as always, to my agent, Sally Holloway, and, above all, to my family.

Quarto

First published in 2025 by Frances Lincoln
an imprint of The Quarto Group.
One Triptych Place, London, SE1 9SH
United Kingdom
T (0)20 7700 9000
www.Quarto.com

EEA Representation, WTS Tax d.o.o.,
Žanova ulica 3, 4000 Kranj, Slovenia
www.wts-tax.si

A catalogue record for this book is available from the British Library.

ISBN 978-1-83600-418-9
EBOOK ISBN 978-1-83600-419-6

10 9 8 7 6 5 4 3 2 1

Book Designer: Wayne Blades
Illustrator: James Oses
Publisher: Philip Cooper
Senior Designer: Isabel Eeles
Senior Editor: Charlotte Frost
Senior Production Manager: Alex Merrett

Printed in Guangdong, China TT062025